DECORATING FOR MODERN LIVING

DECORATING FOR MODERN LIVING

A PRACTICAL, ROOM-BY-ROOM SOURCEBOOK OF IDEAS

Gerd Hatje · Peter Kaspar

TRANSLATED BY ROBERT E. WOLF

HARRY N. ABRAMS INC., PUBLISHERS, NEW YORK

Library of Congress Cataloging in Publication Data

Hatje, Gerd.
  Decorating for modern living.

  Abridged version of the authors' 1601 decorating ideas for modern living, originally published in 1974.
  Includes index.
  1. Interior decoration—Handbooks, manuals, etc.
I. Kaspar, Peter, joint author. II. Title.
NK2115.H34   747'.204   76-48806
ISBN 0-8109-2059-X

Library of Congress Catalogue Card Number 76-48806
All rights reserved. No part of the contents of this book may be reproduced without the written permission of the publishers
HARRY N. ABRAMS, INCORPORATED, NEW YORK
Printed and bound in 1977 in Italy by Arnoldo Mondadori Editore S.p.A., Verona

Contents

Introduction 7

    Making Your Home Your Own 7
    Increased Leisure and Its Consequences 8
    The National Styles 8
    Color in the Home 9

The Entrance 12

    A Place for Coats and a Welcome

The Living Room 20

    A Place to Be Together

Dining Room and Dining Area 62

    A Place for Snacks or Formal Dinner Parties

The Kitchen 72

    To Satisfy the Inner Man

The Bedroom 84

    Comfortable Living Asleep or Awake

Children's Rooms   100
> A Place for Sleep and Play

The Teenager's Room   114
> A Place to Grow Up In

Studies and Hobby Rooms   120
> For Adult Work and Play

The House as a Whole   132
> A Place for Modern Living

Index of Architects and Designers   168

Acknowledgments   168

INTRODUCTION

MAKING YOUR HOME YOUR OWN

The first thing man asks of a place to live in is that it protect him from the outside world, from cold, rain, wind, and hostile intruders—human or animal. Whether man lives in an igloo, wattle hut, or palace, the shelter fulfills the same basic purpose as that more intimate shell, his clothing. Dwelling and clothing have in common the fact that they protect man from an often hostile world. But also, almost as important, they offer him a way to express his *self*, and to indicate the group to which he belongs. To show other people how we see ourselves and what position we claim in society is just as vital as physical security.

The art of making a home involves mastering your own idiom; the technique involves using that idiom in the right place and with the right accents and intonations.

A real home should be a place where the family circle is at ease but where guests and friends also feel welcome. That this has not always been the goal is evidenced by the "salon" of well-to-do nineteenth-century houses, whose counterpart, the more modest "best parlor," has not yet altogether disappeared in some places. What has been gained in informality and comfort by abolishing such stuffy formal rooms must certainly be regarded as progress.

Too often, paradoxically, the more intimate the function, the more anonymous the room. Bedrooms are dominated by a pair of beds lined up side by side and a chest of drawers and dressing table jammed in at random, leaving a minimum of free floor space to maneuver in. Yet there is no reason why a bedroom should not be used as a quiet workplace or as a complement to the living room.

The rhythm of daily life is of the greatest importance in deciding the role of the various areas in the house. Where the ground plan of a home permits various choices—and to the extent that there are no crucial restrictions, such as street noises to be shut out, a pleasant view to be preserved at all costs, access to a balcony, terrace, court, or garden to be considered—the best guide to deciding what each room is to be used for is usually its relation to the points of the compass. The old rules still hold true. Bedrooms should receive morning sun and should therefore face east. A living room is best faced toward the southeast, south, southwest, or west (the last especially if it is used also as an office or studio, in which case it can have the advantage of late afternoon sun). The idea that the kitchen and accessory rooms must face north dates from before the invention of modern refrigeration and air-conditioning, and from an age when kitchens were staffed by servants, for whom the best was deemed far too good. Nowadays it is the housewife who spends the most time indoors, and she has a right to optimum working conditions—to sunlight, good artificial illumination, and step-saving access to living and dining rooms and the children's play areas.

It is also important that the choice of colors be influenced by the natural daylight in a given room. Colors stimulate sensations of warmth or coolness. Experiments have shown that in rooms maintained at exactly the same temperatures but painted with a very warm reddish orange or with an extremely cold color like a bluish green, people tend to over- or underestimate the temperature by as much as five to seven degrees Fahrenheit. Thus, shady rooms should not be made even chillier by cold colors and strongly sunlit rooms should not be made hotter by warm ones.

INCREASED LEISURE AND ITS CONSEQUENCES

The French sociologist Jean Fourastie predicts that by the year 2050 gainful work will demand only 18 percent of our time, as compared with 43 percent in 1880 and 24 percent in 1970. Leisure activities account for the largest percentage of the ways in which people spend their waking hours. Since 70 to 80 percent of free time is spent in the home, this revolution in our lifestyle is already having its effect there.

Increased leisure time is influencing the layout of our homes: there is less demand for separate rooms; "open-plan" dwellings where the family can be together are growing in popularity. Kitchens are no longer connected with dining and living areas by a door or a simple pass-through cut into a wall; they have become an integral part of those areas through the use of open counters or freestanding units. Such solutions, however, demand a considerable gift for organization.

There are, however, aspects of today's home life that do not fit satisfactorily into the open-plan house or apartment. The do-it-yourself trend, for instance, creates problems. The increasingly astronomical fees (and unavailability) of plumbers, carpenters, and house painters force more of us to attempt our own repairs. But those who repair, install, carpenter, or upholster for themselves are likely to want a special room where they can work undisturbed and without distracting their families or neighbors.

However partial one may be to life in one big room, it should be kept in mind that at certain ages nothing can replace a room of one's own. Adolescents want to escape their parents' watchful eye and enjoy things in their own fashion, and the elderly spend their days in a slower rhythm and need more rest. The situation is somewhat different when it comes to small children and their play. The activities of grownups are a constant source of interest to them and a stimulus to their games of make-believe. And when adults have more leisure time they often devote it to their children. The nursery hidden away in an upper story of the house, from which the small fry were permitted to emerge only at set times, is happily a thing of the past. What most families now consider ideal is a children's room large enough for the occasional (invited) parental visit, plus a play area in the general living quarters and, for the smallest, a corner of the kitchen to play in while mother is at work.

It is thus obvious that a good deal of careful planning is required to adapt to individual family circumstances the general principle of combining quite different functions into one room. Without interrupting their flow, the areas devoted to different purposes can be demarcated by simple functional distinctions in their furnishings, by a raised floor, lowered ceiling, or room divider; by well-planned contrasts in either natural or artificial lighting; or by color contrasts. Success lies in balancing the contrasting and unifying elements, in achieving variety within unity. In practical terms, this involves having everything in its place and a place for everything, so that what one does in one area does not interfere with what others do in another.

THE NATIONAL STYLES

Twelve or fifteen years ago it seemed that a few specific tendencies in furniture and interior design were here to stay. With a centuries-old folk tradition behind them, the Scandinavians were producing superbly crafted comfortable and homelike wooden furniture, employing the contrasting textures of such organic materials as wood, rattan, leather, textiles, and fur, all combined with strongly designed and brightly colored accessories. Because of its lack of pretension, the Scandinavian style worked especially well in the small home. In contrast, there were the widely distributed products of a few prestigious American firms which capitalized on precise forms, clean lines, and elegant materials such as chrome, steel, glass or marble, fine veneers or precious woods, and, later, synthetics. A third style was promoted by the Italians: rooms designed with utmost refinement: few but choice pieces of furniture and floors of highly polished marble or ceramic tile, which set a cool and expensive-looking tone.

Today northern Europe has abandoned the folklike style, not only because of changing tastes, but because of the increasing shortage of skilled artisans, carpenters, and cabinetmakers who know what to do with a piece of fine wood. But furniture of polished metal combined with glass, marble, or leather has retained its attraction and is being produced from Chicago to Copenhagen. This style has been given added impetus by the re-creation of the tubular steel furniture designed in the 1920s—the pioneer days of modern design—by men like Marcel Breuer, Mies van der Rohe, and Le Corbusier.

One could hardly speak of national styles today were it not for the Italians. Thanks to the bold initiative of a number of smaller firms, their products have had a triumphal progress comparable only to that of the Scandinavians in the early 1950s. The august Museum of Modern Art in New York has devoted one of the most comprehensive design exhibitions in its history to Italian designers. Recently, the Italians have further developed their concept of the large open landscape for living while at the same time exercising their imagination and technical expertise on individual items, not so much in terms of newly thought-out functions but with a consistent use of splendid colors and freshly conceived forms. Their achievements owe much to plastics, which were originally conceived as a substitute for wood veneers and which soon became a wholly new medium, capable of being molded into ingenious new forms: from their beginning as surface coverings for furniture, they have become the substance of furniture itself.

The countless ideas exported by the Italians in recent years—the very successful bean-bag chair was invented by a team of Italian designers—have been taken up throughout the world. It is a long way from the chaste forms of the Bauhaus days to the mannered free-form sculptures of the present.

As with their attitude toward furniture, most people today are not overly concerned with the puritanical principles of tidiness that dominated room layout up through the international style of the early sixties. Nor is much attention currently paid to those who consider any deviation from strict right angles in the placement of furniture to be anathema. Many people have sloughed off their conservative attitudes and opted for the varicolored chaos of objects now considered chic: sexy posters and striking book and record jackets, table lamps shaped like gargantuan light bulbs, faddish accessories and bric-a-brac, and all the other paraphernalia we seem to require to pass our leisure hours.

Stylistic trends in the fine arts have always had their influence on interior design, but in recent years these trends seem to have merged. Op Art moiré effects are certainly responsible for the fascination of Warren Platner's steel-wire furniture. The large color fields of hard-edge painting have been adopted for interior architecture, often as a way of defining an area of a room without regard for the shapes of walls, windows, and doors, thus making a visual unity independent of function. "Environments"—the interior conceived as a work of art—which have been the concern of many artists since the 1960s, have been nowhere more consistently employed than in the so-called Total Design of the furnishing experts. Nevertheless, the greatest influence on all aspects of current interior design has come from Pop Art, with its cheerful optimism and its unreserved acceptance of a consumer society. Without it we could scarcely have witnessed the revolutionary use of color in the home that is now so widely accepted.

COLOR IN THE HOME

The underlying aesthetic of Pop Art has called into question—even if temporarily—the generally accepted rules regarding the use of color in interior design. Bright and more or less pure colors—especially vital optimistic oranges and fiery aggressive reds—are now seen almost as frequently in homes as on billboards. Nor are strong colors restricted to carpets, draperies, and upholstery; they are being used for the structural elements of furniture as well. It used to be doctrine that one must never place intense colors side by side: now the most brilliant and discordant hues are combined without hesitation. Room designs exploiting closely related hues of the spectrum were always considered risky: today we take in stride bold color schemes that range from vivid green to canary yellow, or from cherry-red to hot orange. For backgrounds we were always advised to depend on neutral whites and grays and muted buffs or browns as the best foil to set off an occasional vivid color accent. Many people ignore this stricture. However, this creates problems when hanging pictures. The paintings, serigraphs, and supergraphics of the 1960s, with their large areas of abstract color, can hold their own against the carnival hues of present-day walls, but subtler pictures have a hard time competing in rooms which are themselves conceived as large-scale color compositions.

Color can also be used to suggest and correct proportions and distances. Through associations in nature, we tend to interpret cool blues and violets as characteristic of hazy distances and warm earth colors as signifying closeness, and we persist in attributing these spatial values to such colors regardless of where we see them, whether in a spectacular sunset or a studio apartment. The advantage in this optical illusion lies in the fact that a room can be made to seem less long and narrow by using a bright color on its far wall, and a low room will seem higher if it is given a cool-colored ceiling. Certain patterns and designs are also useful in reinforcing such illusionistic effects: for example, horizontal stripes can increase a room's length.

Sociologists' inquiries repeatedly show that most people accept their homes as they are. To an astonishing extent they believe that nothing can be done about existing limitations and liabilities, and never even think of alternatives. What appears out of reach is put out of mind.

Yet, as we hope to show in the pages of this book, there are endless ingenious and fascinating ways in which even the most difficult problems can be solved within the limitations imposed by existing architecture, location, and finances. The aim is to create a happier and more comfortable environment, one that fulfills the needs and desires of each member of the family and allows scope for creative expression, relaxation, and growth.

THE ENTRANCE
THE LIVING ROOM
THE DINING ROOM
THE KITCHEN

The Entrance

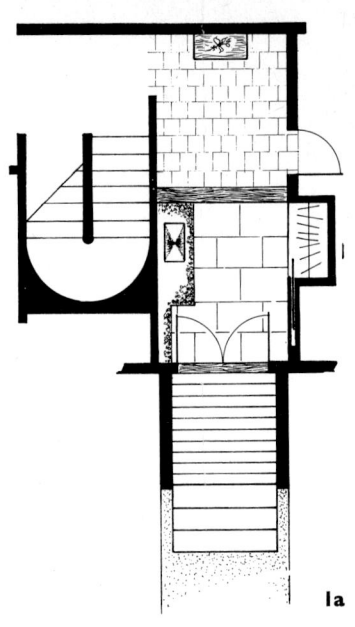

1a

1

2

1   With a refined simplicity verging on the austere and yet with its own kind of excitement, no detail here—not even the careful line-up of the family's slippers—was left to chance. A touch of the Oriental, obvious only in the Japanese flower arrangement on the chest but underlying the entire conception, works hand in hand with the geometrical clarity of modern architectural principles. There is a subtle tension in the contrast between the unadorned wall surfaces and the campaign chest with its ornamental metal fittings. Differences in floor and ceiling levels mark off various sectors in the long entrance hall; these sectors are further emphasized and given a rhythmic sweep by the brick wall and the two types of large floor tiles. The wardrobe is concealed behind the sliding doors to avoid disturbing the clearly balanced spatial effect.

2   A glance and we know that this is the apartment of a passionate art collector. The walls are lined with sheets of plywood over which a coarse linen coated with a special paint is stretched, so that the paintings and drawings can be changed or replaced without leaving ugly nail holes or yellowed patches on the walls. The stone ledge at the left is convenient for small pieces of sculpture. To avoid the annoying reflections and alterations in color caused by direct illumination, spots were sunk flush into the ceiling; their light, reflected by the shiny floor, diffuses throughout the room. The folding doors at the end of the entrance hall open onto the dining room.

The Entrance

3 A simple, practical solution for a workplace in the hall. The writing chest takes up relatively little space and could fit into any but the smallest vestibule. The matching shelving and cabinet units can be used in combination or separately, and can be made to fit into whatever space is available—even the narrow strips of wall between two doors.

4 A bentwood clothes rack and chair make a delicate but graphically precise accent in this hall and harmonize with the overall pastel coloring. The tall, narrow mirror rising from the floor serves to conceal a structural pilaster and also makes the room look larger. The chest in the recess provides a handy place to put visitors' belongings.

The Entrance

5

6

5, 6 These unconventional entrance halls make the best of both practical and formal aspects. In one (plate 5) a false ceiling not only corrects the unfavorable proportions of the room, whose old-fashioned ceiling was much too high, but also provides storage space for trunks and other bulky objects. Looking toward the entrance, the reception area appears deeper than it actually is. Set into dark, intense colors, the white front door appears almost recessed, an impression further emphasized by the prominent door frames in the foreground, which make the entire hall look like a picture. As for the other hall (plate 6), the Louis XVI chest of drawers and the engraving of Whitehall impart a conservative note, but the intense colors create an effect that is anything but conventional. What strikes one immediately is the antique torso, spotlit so that it looms up sharply white against the deep purple wall.

Delight in experimentation is evident in the furnishing of both these halls. Their highly personal and original settings are achieved by improvised means which can easily be changed as fancy dictates. Certainly the front hall is an ideal place to try out new ideas in a new life-style.

7

8

7, 8 This hall creates a decidedly clever and ingenious effect with means ranging from a choice piece of furniture—the Art Deco commode with matching mirror—to a hanging light fixture improvised from a twist of paper. Very effective here (though not necessarily so in a different setting) is the plastic globe lamp sitting directly on the floor. A soft orange lends warmth to the room, and the absence of any other strong color keeps even the motley bright patches in the snakelike carpet from making the room look restless.

9

9 Practical as they are, the recessed washbasin and the tall mirror give real character to this hall. Besides the strong warm colors, note the excellent arrangement whereby light comes from a number of metal-shaded fixtures and is diffused indirectly over wall and ceiling.

16　The Entrance

10

11

10　The serenity here was achieved by synchronizing the various components in terms of both color and form, and by choosing beige as the basic color. The entrance door, coatrack, and shelf are in the same veneer, and the planter, hanging light fixture, and vase have in common a metallic sheen and rather similar design. The coatrack and shelf are fixed to the wall by inconspicuous brackets.

11　Although the general scheme here is open plan, an attempt was made to differentiate the entrance and living areas. The freestanding closet fulfills this task admirably, making a clear division without blocking the spatial flow. On the right-hand side of the closet can be seen some narrow built-in shelves that provide space for books, magazines, and small objects.

12　By using furniture made of transparent synthetic plastics, ▶ even a small front hall can provide all the table and shelf surfaces needed without looking crowded. Brightly colored accessories can enliven such an arrangement, but used in excess they would quickly rob the room of the desired effect of lightness. The coatrack on the recessed far wall could easily have been masked by a hanging, but even a light-colored material would make this room seem smaller. The simple folding coatrack is quite unobtrusive, so that the eye is caught mostly by the transparent cubes and their accessories.

18   The Entrance

13

14

13, 14   Here an alcove was exploited to house a dining table and a two-door built-in closet the left half of which serves as a wardrobe and the right half as a bar within easy reach of the table. The dining equipment can be removed from sight with a minimum of fuss: the table folds up and can be stored in the closet, while the chairs can be stacked. The walls are covered with a white linen and are warmed and softened by its texture. The same linen is used for the tablecloth, giving the room and everything in it a sense of unity.

The Entrance 19

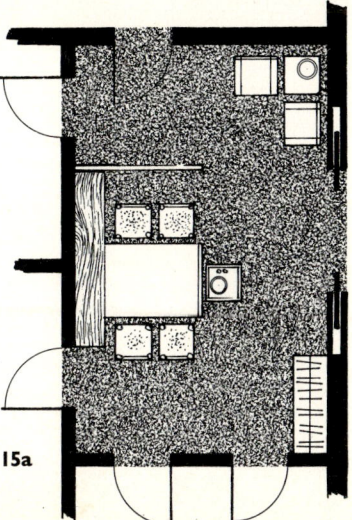

15 The more-than-average dimensions of the entrance hall in this apartment were used to make a dining room and workroom. An openwork room-divider marks off the entrance area and cleverly leads the visitor past the dining area. The large table was constructed from Formica-covered plywood sheets. The narrow counter to the right of the table serves as sideboard but also as a well-lighted sewing or worktable with a small bulletin board above it where notes and patterns and the like can be pinned. Commodious shelves on the wall above can hold books, household items, and a good deal more. With all this there is still room for a small seating area furnished with two armchairs and a table. The three strong basic colors—red, white, and blue—are repeated even in the table setting. The red-enameled walls are almost mirror-like and make the room seem even larger.

The Living Room

◀ 16 A well-defined and carefully balanced seating area in an American house. The focus of the relatively small room is the fireplace, whose architectural simplicity is further emphasized by the subtle geometry of the painting by Josef Albers hanging above it. The furniture is arranged in relation to the fireplace, and the floor lamps (one on either side of the fireplace) fit neatly into the overall symmetrical composition. The wall, lined with books, acts as foil and complement to the large window recess opposite. Uniform rows of shelves are broken up by a Robert Indiana print, the bold tones of which strike the only sharp accent in the room's otherwise muted color scheme. Both pictures are illuminated by lights in the ceiling; the standing lamps cast their light downward.

17, 18 Although this living room is in an old house in Paris, it is an example of superb contemporary interior design. Only the windows behind the vertical translucent louvers, which fit in beautifully with these streamlined furnishings, have been left unaltered. Seating accommodations are spread across the entire width of the room, but to avoid separating the armchairs and sofa unduly, the room was narrowed by the folding screen, which stands out like a carved relief against the black background (plate 18). In the rear of the room (plate 17) there is a reading nook with two floor-to-ceiling bookcases and a dramatically sculpturesque spiral staircase made of prefabricated metal components. The color tonalities of the travertine floor and the rug in the seating area are quite similar and provide a restful background for the strong orange of the sofa, armchair, and screen.

17

18

22 The Living Room

19 An insistence on formal symmetry characterizes this living room, whose muted beige and white tones create a reserved, dignified atmosphere in which the only forceful accent comes from the deep red of the hard-edge painting at left. The two Oriental-style coffee tables and the Louis XV bergère armchairs introduce a note of relaxation in the otherwise clearly organized room. According to the number of guests, the armchairs can be moved to make a small group with a single sofa or a larger one with both sofas.

20 The furniture here is brought right up to the traditional fireplace with its overmantel mirror. By keeping the sofa, small coffee table, and fireplace all in white, they are set off as a unit which stands out against the black walls where the old stucco molding has been painted an elegant white.

21 Here the unfavorable proportions of the room have been cleverly played down. A long, narrow alley, the room allowed for only a continuous L-shaped couch, which bridges the jutting pilaster, so that now the eye takes in the two parts of the room as one.

The Living Room

22 This seating group arranged around a coffee table is sunk two steps below the floor level, thereby acquiring a special feeling of intimacy. The dark brown of the carpet, which continues up the stairs to cover the rest of the room, makes a splendid background for the gray sofas and the yellow and brown cushions. A note of informality is achieved by the casual placement of the pictures. Not to be overlooked is the amusing contrast in style between the painting by De Chirico in the corridor at the rear and the Op Art favored in the living room.

The stereo is housed with considerable ingenuity. The cabinets at the rear hold the tape recorder, record player, and amplifier. Behind the vertical grilles at the right and the left are the loudspeakers. Although plainly visible, the equipment is not obtrusive. On the other hand, the four large bouquets on the coffee table are too much of a good thing in this otherwise beautifully conceived room, and block one's view of people seated opposite.

24 The Living Room

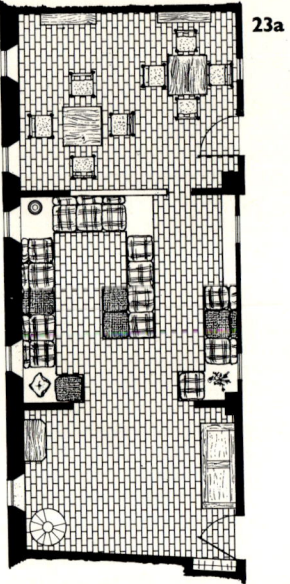

23

23 In remodeling, a good deal of the original character of this onetime farmhouse was preserved, and even the existing division of the room was retained in the new living room. In the rear, a dining area is set off from the rest of the room by a low partition; this partition also serves as a backrest for the large cushions placed on the plastered masonry platform that takes the place of a conventional couch and easy chairs. The quiet beige and brown cushions combine harmoniously with the color of the old brick-tile flooring. Bright color accents are provided by the lamps, artificial flowers, pillows, and paintings. In the immediate foreground is the entrance hall, from which a circular staircase leads to the upper story.

23a

24

24 Here, too, the seating area—a low platform around a fireplace—takes its form from the architecture itself. In this luxurious city apartment, however, it is accomplished with considerably more refinement. The fine quality of the materials and the use of only black and white create a more elegant and also more formal setting (one which may, indeed, strike some as rather austere).

The Living Room

25, 26 Two rooms entirely without the usual seating accommodations. Informal cushions encourage improvised and spontaneous groupings, though not the last word in comfortable sitting. In the more spacious room (plate 25) a platform of various levels was built into a corner to divide the fireplace zone from the rest of the room. The cushions, piled up so decoratively here, can be scattered about freely in front of the fireplace. The smaller room (plate 26), in a bachelor's home, is simple and unpretentious. Tables and ledges are kept to a height in keeping with the cushion seats on the floor.

27 This spacious living room takes its cue chiefly from the architecture itself, dispensing almost entirely with movable furniture. It achieves its effect by the exciting contrast of the cool-looking tile floor and whitewashed stone wall against the softness and warmth suggested by the materials used in the seating area and the ceiling. The broad conversation pit is oriented toward the dominant fireplace and is lighted by spotlights in the ceiling; no lamps break up the smooth spatial flow of the room as a whole.
See overleaf for illustration

25

26

26 The Living Room

27

28

27 *See preceding page for caption*

28 A sunken area in front of the fireplace makes up the core of this living room, with the two steps leading into it providing additional seating space. The color scheme—pale olive green and white—contributes to the peaceful atmosphere of this room, which is open to nature on three sides.

29 Here the entire room becomes an elegantly ▶ laid-out seating area on four different levels. The depression in the center is surrounded by a number of different comfortable seating possibilities—cushions and backrests set against the rear wall, backed or backless cushions on the platforms, and so on. The picture set into the floor breaks up the mass of red and gives a visual focus to the sunken area.

28 The Living Room

30

30 In this bookcase wall, five square compartments framed in travertine house the fireplace, wood supply, and bar, among other things. Because the compartments are all the same size, the fireplace does not call attention to itself, but remains just another part of the wall.

31 Bold architectural features largely set the character of this room. The materials—raw stained wood for the walls, brick for the fireplace—lend a rustic yet refined note which is played against the textures and colors used for the seating group. Because of the light upholstery and carpet, the group holds its own in this dramatic setting, and the well-padded couches do not seem heavy despite their considerable bulk. The transparency of the table top and base gives the area in front of the fireplace an open and spacious feeling. The arrangement of the seating group is excellent—although it is immediately related to the fireplace, it does not face directly into the opening, but is instead linked with the outdoors through the large windows.

The Living Room

32

32 In contrast to the preceding example with its precisely organized arrangement, this room is characterized by easygoing improvisation that relies on inherent good taste. Though the furniture and accessories are anything but unified in style, it is precisely their polyglot character that accounts for the pleasant and very personal informality we feel here. The focus of the seating arrangement around the fireplace is the heavy wooden coffee table. A brightly colored patterned rug joins the sofa, armchair, and table into a single unit and, at the same time, sets it off from the rest of the room. The wicker chair in the corner is easily drawn up for additional visitors. Small red cushions on the windowsill and a hanging lamp transform the niche into a reading nook. In the background one looks through to the dining room and kitchen.

The Living Room 31

33

34

33 Here is an example of how a more traditional fireplace, such as we saw in plate 20, can be transformed to fit into a modern setting. Painted over in black, the sculptural details of an earlier age become less noticeable and make a background for the very original up-to-date version of the old-fashioned overmantel mirror.

34 Because of the mirror effect of its slightly curved stainless-steel surfaces, this fireplace has all the quality of a piece of kinetic sculpture or some splendidly conceived and realized product of industrial engineering design. This impression is furthered by a lighting system that utilizes movable spots attached to a track suspended from the ceiling. The comfortable seats along the wall are mounted on a continuous platform of steel, and the other furnishings are kept in the same clear and rigorous key.

The Living Room

35 A single continuous slab holds both fireplace and leather-cushioned benches in this house in the Danish countryside. There are leather cushions for additional seating. The overmantel, like the walls and bench, is painted white, so that the fireplace, rather than becoming the showpiece of the room, is only another inconspicuous component of the seating area.

36 This freestanding fireplace in white-painted concrete combines with a low divider to separate the entrance from the seating area. The broad mantel has room for the tape recorder, record player, and amplifier; the divider makes a handy shelf and is the right height for an end table. While a full-scale wall could have been used as a partition here, the open-plan solution makes the area appear roomier.

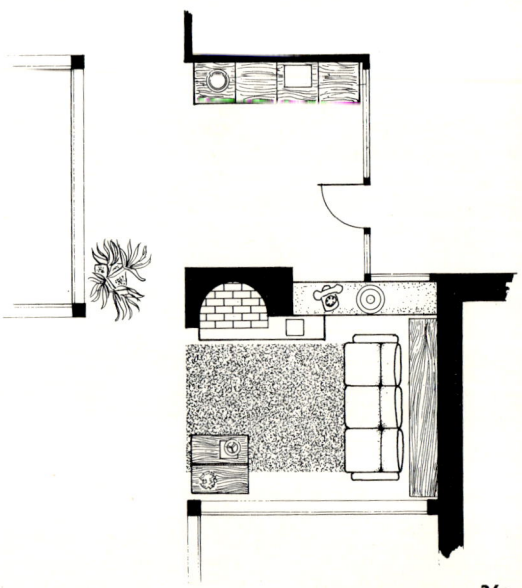

37 The fireplace in this New York apartment has been made into the equivalent of a piece of sculpture and is the most prominent feature of the room. The deliberately sloppy manner in which it is painted acts as a sophisticated foil to the rigorous step-pyramid of the hood and base, and its form and color are echoed in the large painting on the adjacent wall.

38 The fireplace and the wall behind it combine here into a single three-dimensional pictorial composition. The base and flue form a continuous column, opening out at seating level to accommodate the hearth.

34 The Living Room

39

39 This lively juxtaposition of boxlike units made with consummate craftsmanship from a number of different woods holds not only books and art objects but also the most-used items of tableware for the adjacent dining area. Such solutions can be achieved with the most elementary means—even packing cases of the same size stacked above and alongside each other. And, as the bookcase wall grows, the irregular layout and the spaces between one box and the next will still look light and informal even when, with the years, it becomes tightly packed with books.

40 Given an extremely narrow room, this is an unpretentious and comfortable way to arrange a seating area and bookshelves. None of the sturdy wooden shelves extend across the entire width of the wall, and the gaps create pleasing variations.

The Living Room

41 A bookcase with shelves designed to allow for a sloping ceiling makes a striking rear wall for this room. The rows of books are pleasantly varied by colorful plates, vases, and jars. The worktable is the same height as the lowest shelf, which thus supplies an often-needed additional working surface.

42 This very light and open combination desk and bookcase is constructed of thin metal rods joined to support glass shelves. At table height a broad working surface has been provided, and the two drawers at the left, also suspended from the rods, hold stationery and other supplies.

The Living Room

43

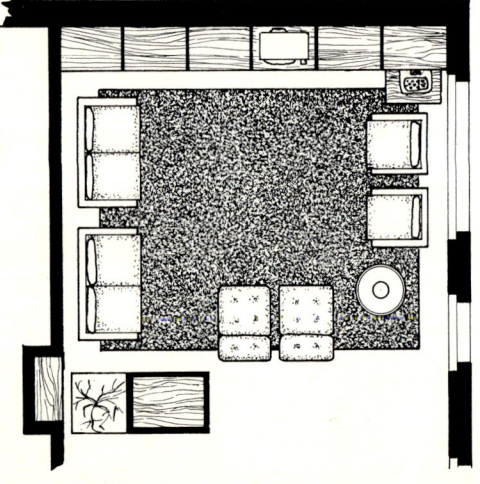

43a

43 The expanse of bookcases here sets the character of the room. A number of cabinets house everything needed—stereo, television, bar, a writing cabinet opening out on hinges—enabling the rest of the room to be furnished rather sparsely. The speakers encased in Plexiglas, with all their technical components exposed, make a dramatic contrast to the straight lines of the bookcase itself; they are beamed at the two Eames armchairs in the foreground, which are placed there for optimum reception.

44 A freestanding pillar the height of the room fulfills many functions: on one side a built-in bar with a small tabletop also used for meals; on another side shelves to display collector's items; on a third side a brace supporting a writing table in the cleverly devised workplace behind it. Thus, what might otherwise be an eyesore becomes a highly effective room divider and screens off the work area from the dining area. The openness of the room is scarcely interrupted, yet anyone using the workplace has a feeling of privacy.

38 The Living Room

45 A large room can be divided into living area and study by a bookcase wall. Here, in order not to lose all relationship between the two zones, two glass display cases were built into the wall; their white framing makes them stand out like windows connecting one area with the other. The density of the dividing wall is further mitigated by the single white-painted shelf unit which, together with the white door panel below it, creates a tall vertical axis reaching from floor to ceiling.

45

The Living Room 39

46

47

46, 47 To provide for a very large library in this house, an entire wall of the living room and even the door to the bedroom (plate 47) were lined with shelves. The idea of utilizing even the door surface goes back to the old Baroque libraries and is transposed here into modern terms. The steady succession of shelves is broken only by the vertical strip of window (plate 46) and the two sections for displaying collector's items. The rest of the furnishings are equally well thought out—the long storage cabinet, for example, marks off the writing and reading area from the fireplace zone with its seating group.

40 The Living Room

48   Starting with a long rectangular room, part of the terrace was glassed off to create interior space for a dining area. The light, simple furnishings make this annex appear quite open, so that terrace and dining space still seem to make a single room, an impression reinforced by the use of the same color for the rug in the dining area and the matting on the terrace.

48

49   A sofa set across the room separates the seating and dining ▶ areas without creating a visual obstruction. The mixture of styles in the spacious seating group centered on the tubular copper chimney hood strikes a happy note of informality which contrasts with the more unified effect of the dining table and matching chairs.

50   An example of how important it is to divide logically ▶ whatever space you have, especially in smaller rooms. Instead of making use of the entire width of the room, the couches and side tables are drawn close together, leaving the corner free for a reading nook. The division is further emphasized by a large suspended cabinet which contains the bar.

49

50

42 The Living Room

51

51–53 At first glance this living room in an old Parisian house seems to have acquired its present appearance without much forethought and planning. A second look, however, shows that much refinement went into the furnishings. The beamed ceiling and the fireplace wall (plate 51) were painted white, while the remaining walls and the floor are done in a warm brown which, in turn, contrasts with the white of the conversation group (plate 52). With a few easy manipulations, the L-shaped couch converts into a guest bed. The Art Nouveau-style vases seem to have been arranged at random, but the lighting and the way their colors harmonize with the wall prove this is not so. A low two-tier table does double duty, providing a handy shelf or table top and also defining the seating area. With its light chrome supports and glass top, the small writing table between the windows is inconspicuous and airy (plate 53). The two bookcases are not built in, but are held in their niches by metal floor-to-ceiling fixtures.

The Living Room 43

52

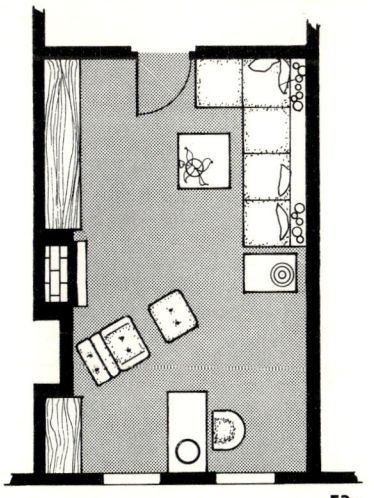
53a

53

44 The Living Room

54

55 56

54–57 Another old house in Paris that was done over. An extremely limited space was exploited for a combined living room and sleeping quarters, with furnishings that masterfully overcome all handicaps. The long couch converts into two beds (plate 55). The table pulls out of the wall and seats four for dining (plate 56); it also serves as a writing table or sideboard (plate 57). The mantel makes a handy bar. The walls and fireplace are enameled in deep blue, a color especially attractive at night, and one that makes the room seem unified and intimate. Only the two sofas, with their bright red upholstery, stand out prominently (plate 54), while the small, light glass-and-chrome tables are scarcely more obtrusive than a subtle, sketchy outline. The lamps are placed directly on the floor.

The Living Room

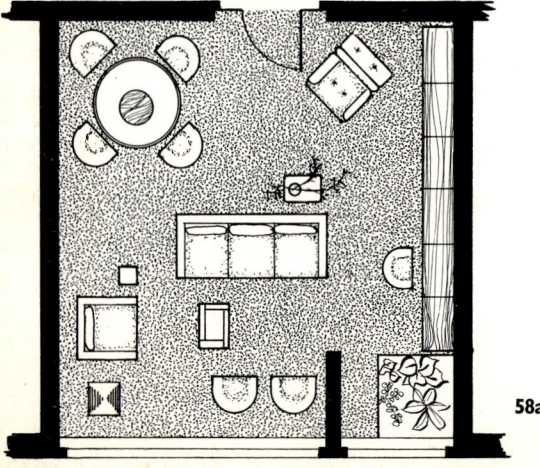

58 With the simplest of means, this room has been inconspicuously but firmly divided into a lounging and a dining area. The hanging bamboo mat, the yellow lamp, and the large vermilion Japanese vase holding a bare branch combine into an attractive Oriental composition, giving visual focus and spatial definition to the leather sofa standing free in the room. In the evening, by the yellow light of the lamp, the bizarre silhouette of the branch is most dramatic. One wall was left in bare brick, and its rustic character is perhaps somewhat out of tune with the other furnishings. The bookcase, with its black supports and shelves and discreet workplace, scarcely stands out against the brick background. In short, an excellent example of a room that is spacious and open and yet takes on new form from a well-placed partition.

The Living Room

59

60

59, 60   In this large room the living-room area is separated from the dining and work area by double-sided bookcases and a blind of movable vertical strips which offer a number of possibilities for breaking up space and are attractive in themselves. The light-gray carpeting in both parts of the room creates a visual link and helps play down the actual division. Brightly patterned peasant rugs lend prominence to the dining area (plate 60) and the workplace (plate 59). The writing table is fixed to the bookcase in front of the window, where it gets direct daylight. The small dining table is part of a continuous wall ledge and can be pulled out at mealtimes.

48 The Living Room

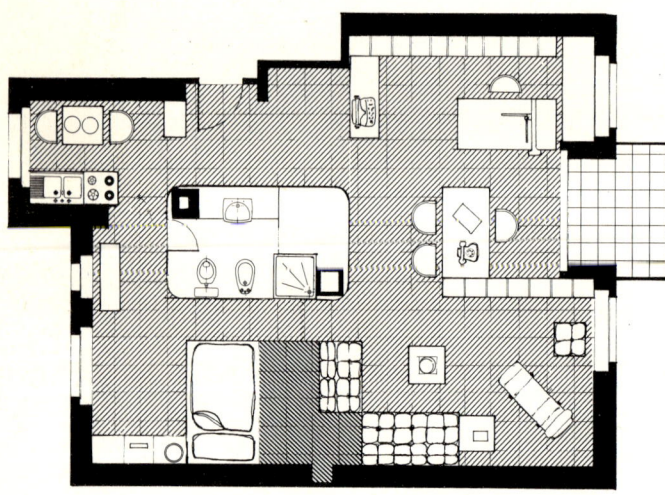

61

61a

61–63 When new bathroom facilities were built into the center of this apartment, an otherwise completely open area was modified. From entrance to sleeping area, the individual zones succeed each other continuously and almost without distinction. This feature is underscored by the use of black and white as basic colors, relieved only by accessories and the books on the shelves. The floor and the walls of the bathroom unit are covered with extremely durable industrial-quality rubber tiles (plate 62). From the open entrance the large yellow design on the bathroom unit's wall carries the eye into the living area (plate 63). One passes through an extensive working area with various work tables (plate 63), one of which can also be used for dining, to arrive at the seating area, which is clearly defined by a half-height bookcase low enough not to interrupt the spatial flow of the room. Both this and the wall bookcase are constructed of open aluminum cubes joined by brackets and easily assembled and disassembled. Since the aluminum backing can also be rearranged at will, some shelves have been closed off on the side facing the seating group and are open on the other side (plate 61). The low bookcase and the sofa placed crosswise nicely define the seating area in the corner and mark it off from the workplace and sleeping quarters.

The Living Room 49

62

63

The Living Room

64

65

64–67 This large living room is divided into seating and dining areas by a freestanding pillar containing a fireplace, and also by a suspended segment of wall attached at a right angle to the fireplace unit (plate 66). Despite their severe forms, the fireplace unit and wall segment make a lively three-dimensional composition. The open areas below and to the right of the suspended wall afford interesting views, and people in the seating area are not isolated from the rest of the room. Deep violet and blue dominate in the bookcases, a portion of dropped ceiling, and certain walls (plate 67), while in the dining area the light beige walls and the bright-red upholstery of the chairs strike quite a different note (plate 65). The contrast in color emphasizes the division of the room and creates two distinct environments: a small, bright daylight zone including the dining area and the window wall (plates 65, 66), and a large seating area whose strong, dark colors come into their own only by artificial light (plate 67). In a corner adjacent to the window wall, a smaller seating group provides a comfortable place for listening to music or watching television (plate 64).

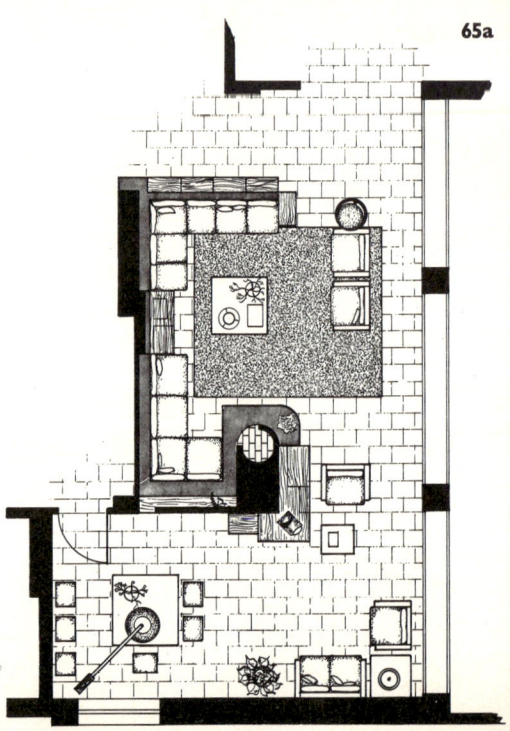

65a

The Living Room

The Living Room

68

68, 69 In this apartment in the heart of old Milan, a large library was installed in the living room. The floor plan offered a long rectangular main area and a clearly subordinate adjoining extension. No doubt this plan could have been exploited quite differently by assigning the living area to the long part of the room and relegating the dining area to the small extension. Instead, the space was divided by placing a sofa crosswise, leaving only a narrow passage to the library area, which was raised two steps above floor level (plate 69), and in which only minor importance was conceded to the dining facilities: the table on the right also serves as a dining table. All three walls of the library are lined with built-in bookcases which make good use of every inch of space. Because of their uniform height and white color, the effect is discreet and neutral. The left-hand entrance to the room is framed with bookshelves, and the windows opposite are hung with white draperies set into broad moldings, so that there seems to be virtually no break in the bookcase walls.

The chest behind the sofa also serves as a buffet. In the main room the floor level is reserved for the seating group, from which, unblocked by the backless upholstered divan, there is a splendid view of the great Romanesque church of Sant' Ambrogio through the large picture window (plate 68). One end of the bookcase wall extends and, with the door to the terrace, defines the music corner with the grand piano (plan 69a). Alongside the couch a custom-built cabinet holds the phonograph and part of the record collection.

The Living Room 53

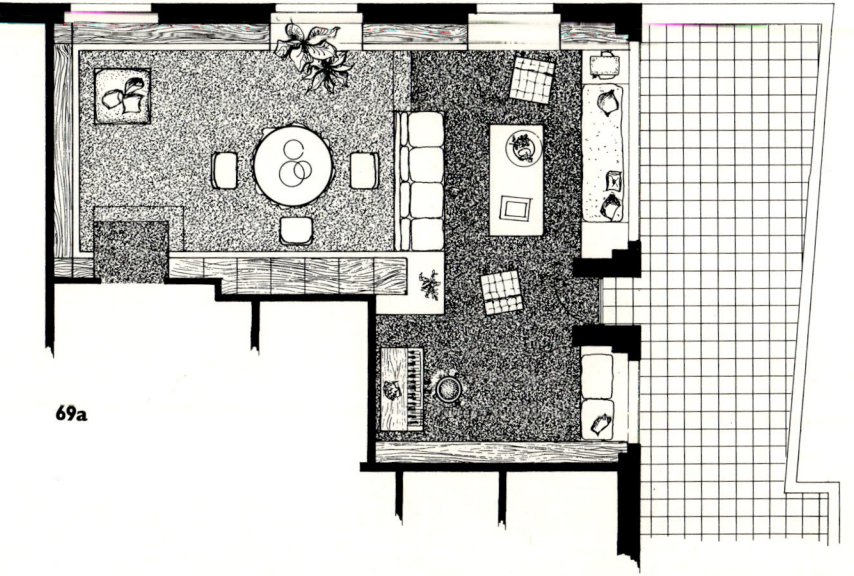

69

69a

54 The Living Room

70 Here a different level goes with a different function. The dining table is placed on a high platform near the kitchen. Lest this difference in height make too sharp a separation, both levels have the same floor covering, and the cabinet and shelf units are carried over from one level to the other. The unusual armchairs are easily converted into beds and go well with this unconventional interior.

The Living Room

71

72

71, 72 The front of the platform in this living room recess is hinged so it can be used for storing bed linens and even quite bulky objects. The seating area promotes relaxed sociability, replacing conventional chairs and couches with loose cushions and a large mattress. The platform also serves to correct the proportions of a very narrow room, the height of which is greater than its width.

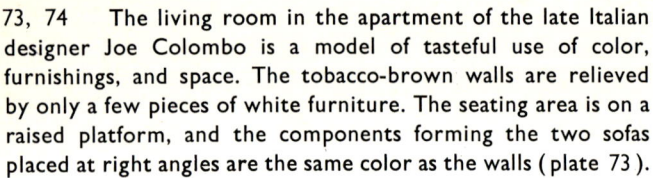

73

73, 74 The living room in the apartment of the late Italian designer Joe Colombo is a model of tasteful use of color, furnishings, and space. The tobacco-brown walls are relieved by only a few pieces of white furniture. The seating area is on a raised platform, and the components forming the two sofas placed at right angles are the same color as the walls (plate 73).

The tabletop at the lip of the platform is movable and can be used as a low coffee table accessible from the couch or become a dining table when placed over the lower part of the room (plate 74). The lights can be adjusted to cast good light on the table in either position.

74

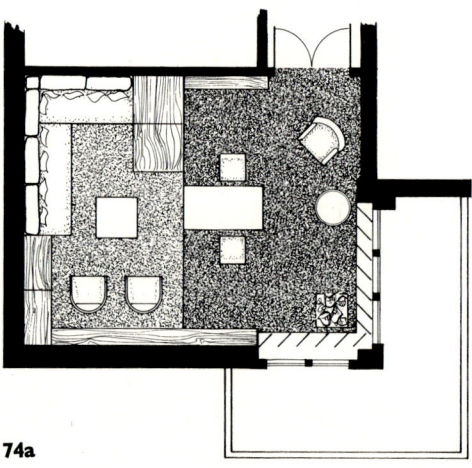

74a

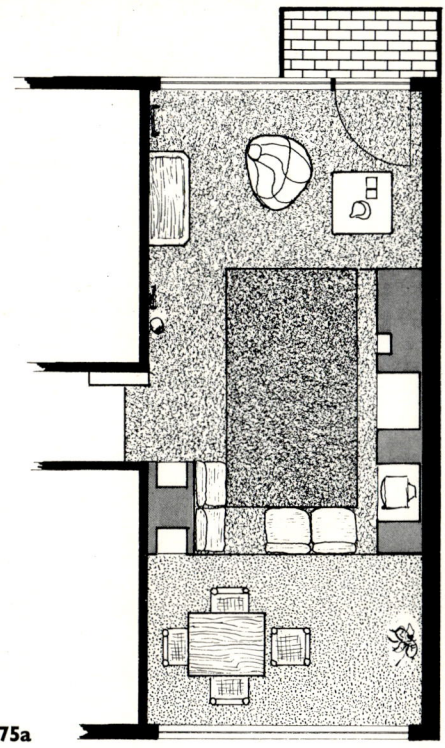

75a

75

76

75, 76 In remodeling a conventional apartment, two previously separate rooms were opened into a single long room. A platform built by the owner himself extends through the entire living room to divide it into three zones: a sunken seating area in the center, a reading area at an intermediate height along the far window wall (plate 75), and a dining area at the opposite end of the room, which is raised still higher (plate 76). The platform of the dining area makes a backrest for the cushions of the conversation pit. To correct the unsatisfactory proportions of the narrow room, a false ceiling in natural wood was built over the seating area. The usual sideboards, tables, and chests were replaced by a few built-in cabinets whose alternating projections and recesses create an interesting diversity. One such niche is used for the television set, which is placed directly on the floor at the correct eye level for the seating area. Above it, glass shelves hold books, magazines, and small objects. The adjoining niche houses the stereo components. All in all, a very livable and original solution, in which the unconventional elements do not strive to be "modern," yet create a bold spatial effect.

58 The Living Room

77 In a broadly conceived open-plan room there can be two separate seating groups which, while very different, complement each other nicely. Here the one on the upper level is designed for relaxed companionship in small groups. The dark, warm brown; the low ceiling; and the pinpoint spotlighting—all conspire to create an intimate atmosphere further underscored by the wall of books and the tiny white-enamel coal stove. Quite unlike this upper area, the large conversation group at floor level is much more formal, with light uniform upholstery, a rigorously symmetrical layout, and accessory furniture based on variants of the cube. The main room offers a number of possibilities for variation. In normal circumstances the dining and seating areas are clearly separated by a room divider in opaque yellow plastic with a sculpture placed in front of it. For large gatherings the divider is removed, the sculpture and dining chairs shifted to the side, and the two armchairs put beside the sofa to make a large open room (plan 77a).

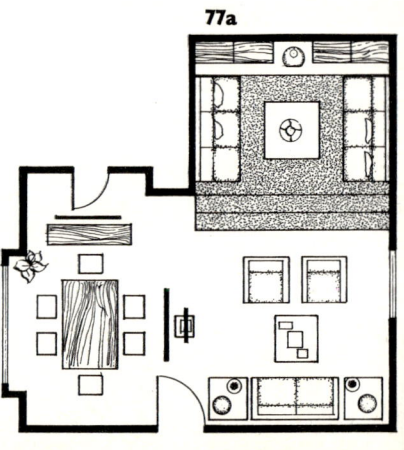

78

78 This remarkable apartment is in an old Parisian house. Built in the seventeenth century, the house had been remodeled repeatedly through the years. The original beamed ceiling was incorporated into a coffered one with a geometrical effect emphasized even more by subtly outlining the inside of each of the coffers in black. Other elements suggestive of a historical style—notably the nineteenth-century moldings and the doors—were left unaltered. Into this new-old setting were introduced unusual materials—steel, Plexiglas, and synthetics—which, together with forceful contrasts of black and white, unorthodox furnishings, and a fine collection of abstract geometrical and kinetic art, give the room its contemporary look. Most of the floor was given over to an off-white-carpeted platform that serves as a base for three sofas. The huge wave-shaped sectional couch with small tables makes a lively counterpoint to the otherwise rigorous right angles of the room. Two large smoked Plexiglas panels project about three feet into the room and shorten it. While the artworks on the other walls are restricted to black-and-white, the glowing colors of the two by Victor Vasarely stand out with special vividness against the panels' neutral gray background.

79
79a

79–82 By the use of whites and browns, carefully calculated furniture groupings, and the placement of individual objects, the spaciousness of this room in a New York apartment is handsomely emphasized. Strong colors and additional furniture would have produced an entirely different effect. Because of its array of glassware and the mirrored wall behind it, the bar cabinet (plan 79a) in the middle of the room appears lighter than its dimensions would lead one to expect, and it divides the area without breaking the spatial flow. It also serves as a clever disguise for a structural pillar. The seating group (plate 79), with its white couches on a rug of almost the same shade, takes its place harmoniously in the overall architectural setting. The fireplace is set flush into the wall, without any attempt to dress it up. The large coffee table was brought close to the lefthand sofa because it would have been too difficult to reach in the center, and the other couch can be served by the light occasional table. Indirect light comes from ledges flanking the fireplace and from the plastic pillar floor lamp. In the rest of the room, good illumination is supplied by spots sunk into the ceiling. The only "furniture" in the otherwise empty entrance hall is an old scale mounted on a white pedestal, which stands out starkly in this setting. The relief on the back wall of the bar (plate 80), like all the works of art, testifies to the owners' love for abstract geometrical art. In front of the built-in bookcase (plate 81) there is a second and smaller seating area for reading or relaxing, separated from the main one by two leather-cushioned Mies van der Rohe stools, which can be incorporated when needed into one or the other of the two groups.

The dining area is in an adjoining open area carpeted in a light color. The sideboard unit (plate 82) backed with a mirror makes the room look larger and helps minimize the contrast between the openness of the living area and the relatively closed-in dining area.

80

81

82

62 Dining Room and Dining Area

83

83 This dining room opens on the garden and is linked with it by a handsome arrangement of plants. The furniture is sober and practical, restricted to a dining table and four leather chairs on chrome steel frames. The Op Art relief framed in a shallow wall niche and lighted by built-in spots goes well with the restrained modernity of the room as a whole. The floor covering matches the basic colors of the two pictures.

84 In a room as sparsely furnished as this, every detail must be coordinated or minor defects that would pass unnoticed in a "busier" setting become painfully obvious. The open sweep of picture windows and the white ceiling is countered by dark-gray slate flooring and brown-and-black patterned wallpaper, a contrast carried over to the furniture—white chairs with black cushions around a smoked-glass table. In such a neutral setting, the wallpaper with its pronounced Liberty-type pattern does very nicely. In front of the smaller windows, Art Nouveau vases and glasses have been arranged in a subtle composition on narrow glass shelves. The window ledges are slabs of light-colored marble, and one is used as a serving counter. The airy feeling of the room is increased by the absence of lamps and chandeliers; the illumination is provided by concealed light strips along the tops of the walls and can be regulated by a dimmer.

Dining Room and Dining Area

88 An open area between the kitchen and living room offered enough space here for a dining table and chairs. The kitchen can be closed off by a light curtain, but the dining area remains open to the living room and is therefore furnished in the same style and with the same wall-to-wall carpeting. The storage wall behind the dining table is used for tableware and glasses, and the open shelves make a handy serving counter.

89 A large room next to the kitchen serves here as both dining and workroom. The dining area is by the wall leading to the kitchen. The workplace—for which good light is needed—is set up along the large window wall. The shelving extends over the door to the living room and provides a colorful note through the contrast of yellow cabinets and shelves with the dark-brown wooden framework. The latter continues throughout the room as simple strip molding at floor and ceiling level. Since both the work and dining tables have dark legs and yellow tops, the room acquires a marked formal unity.

88

89

Dining Room and Dining Area 65

87 The very formal and decidedly elegant setting is almost overemphasized by the mirror wall, with its illusionistic effect of depth, which makes what is already a large room appear almost barnlike. Thanks to the graceful table and chairs, the dining area fits discreetly into this stately setting, with its black walls relieved by white stucco molding.

64   Dining Room and Dining Area

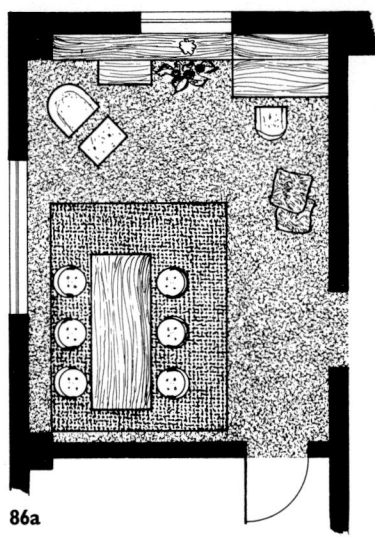

86a

85   86

85, 86   To accommodate a small writing table or study area into a dining room, it helps to shift the dining table to a corner rather than leave it in its conventional position in the middle of the room. Although there are two distinct areas here, the portion reserved for dining is emphasized by its Chinese rug and excellent furnishings, and thus is made to dominate and set the tone of the entire room. The hinged writing shelf is part of the built-in bookcase and attracts little attention. The furnishings—bentwood chairs, an old French table, a chandelier, a Chinese rug, a wall-size eighteenth-century map of Rome—were selected with unerring taste, and the contemporary picture on the far wall of the dining area offers a most original variation on the decorative sweep of the Thonet chairs.

Dining Room and Dining Area

90, 91 Here the living room, dining room, and kitchen open into each other but can be quickly closed off by an accordion door—which, when closed, fits into a wall cabinet—and by a Venetian blind which can be let down over the dividing counter. The kitchen (plate 90) receives daylight through a window wall that extends from the dining area to the seating group in the living room (plate 91). A freestanding counter serves both as work surface and buffet. Furnished with light bentwood chairs and a Saarinen dining table with white metal base and pale-gray marble top, the dining area does not look cramped despite its very limited space, and the narrow lithograph by Joan Miró adds to the sense of space.

90

91

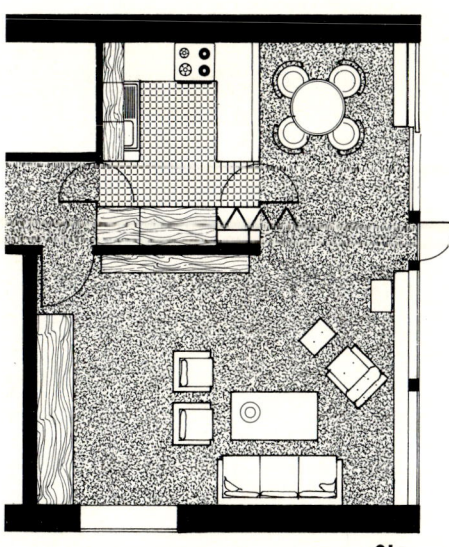

91a

68 Dining Room and Dining Area

92

92   Kitchen and dining area here are separated by a wood-paneled partition. The serving hatch with its chrome frame and white sliding doors stands out strikingly against the wooden wall and, beyond practical considerations, serves to break up the large flat surface in an interesting fashion. With walls, table, and chairs all in the same wood, the dining area takes on a satisfyingly unified appearance.

93   A shelf unit open on both sides makes a practical room divider. Within easy reach of the kitchen, the tableware can be placed on the shelves after washing, then removed from the other side at mealtimes. With all storage and serving problems thus nicely solved, no more is needed in the dining area than this plain wooden table with two benches, which afford plenty of room to seat a large family.

93

Dining Room and Dining Area

94 In this kitchen, like the one we have just seen, a shelf unit separates the cooking and dining zones. The latter gets direct daylight from a second window. The kitchen was designed for practicality, with gray tile flooring, glazed tile walls, and built-in cabinets and fixtures. In contrast, the dining area, with its light carpeting, plants, and books in an open bookcase, is quietly domestic in feeling. Although they make only a minor interruption in the room, the open shelves successfully create a certain distance between the busy world of the kitchen and the restfulness of the dining area.

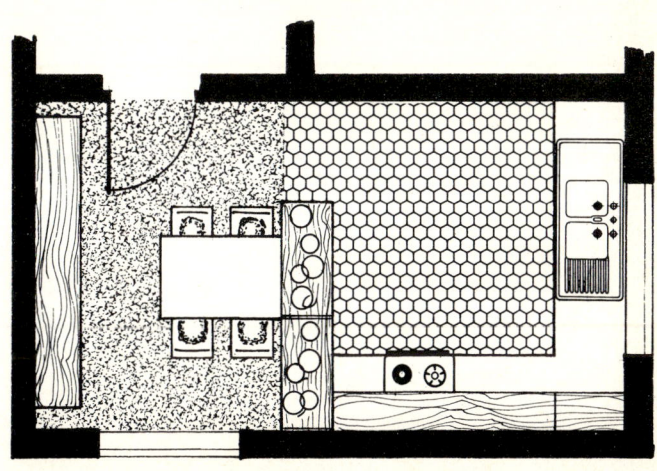

70 Dining Room and Dining Area

95 Space was lacking for a proper division here, so the cooking zone was made as unobtrusive as possible, with walls and cabinets all in white to make a uniform surface. The Andy Warhol lithograph, the carpeting, the swivel lamp, the hanging light, and the pleasant furniture contrive to give the room a cozy feeling without interfering with the practical requirements of a well-run kitchen.

Dining Room and Dining Area 71

96 Four bar stools and a built-in tabletop between kitchen and living area add up to an efficient place for breakfast, lunch, and snacks.

96

97

97 This small kitchen was set up with the precision of a modern laboratory. Breakfast area, work surfaces, and stove are combined into a single block lighted and ventilated from the same overhead unit. The highly polished metal stools can be stowed out of the way in the open recess beneath the breakfast counter.

The Kitchen

98 Between the work counter and the wall to the living room there is only a narrow passage, but despite the limited space, all the necessities are well taken care of, thanks to ingenious use of built-ins. The sink and stove are mounted in a large white-topped counter, which not only provides a good deal of working surface but also has roomy drawers and cabinets below it. These, like the open shelves above, are in natural wood.

99 With its brown cabinet fronts, the brown ceramic mosaic tiles of the floors and walls, and the work counter in laminated wood, this Parisian kitchen is an example of good design which includes all the practical necessities. Standing in front of the stove—which can be pulled out to make it easier to reach the back burners—one need only turn around to reach the sink. Drawers, trash bin, and spice and condiment bottles are all at hand. The oven is not together with the burners but instead is built into the cupboard wall at a height which does away with stooping. The dining area directly adjoins the kitchen.

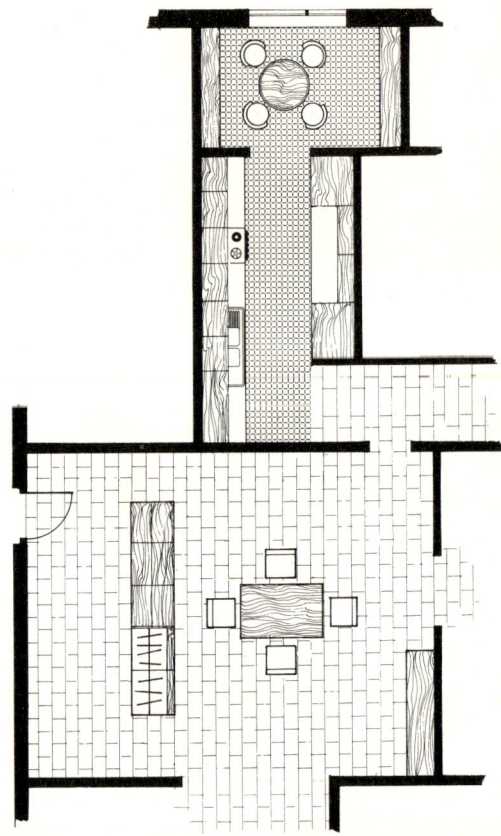

The Kitchen 73

100

101

100, 101 Two kitchens with almost identical floor plans and furnishings: the sink and stove are combined on the right to make a common working area, and the built-in cabinets are set up in an L-shape in front of the window and the right wall. In one kitchen, however, the opposite wall is used for a large built-in unit incorporating the oven and grill (plate 100); thus, with less wall space available, the breakfast table was set on casters to be rolled out as needed. In the other kitchen (plate 101), built-in cabinets were not required, and the room is in consequence lighter and more airy. The small table is hinged to the wall and can be dropped down out of the way.

102

102 In a large kitchen the basic components can be placed in the middle of a wall to make a U-shaped working unit with proportions which are ideal, both practically and aesthetically. The rest of the room is thus left free for a dining area or even for a play area. Here a breakfast nook was set up on one side of the work counter.

74 The Kitchen

103 Located in the interior of the house, this large kitchen is at an equal distance from the small breakfast area and the formal dining room. Natural light comes indirectly from the picture window and glass door and directly from a large skylight. To emphasize the connection between breakfast area and kitchen, both rooms were given the same gleaming floor covering. The generous working surfaces are lighted by fluorescent tubes on the underside of the wall cabinets, a solution which provides good light without obliging the cook to work in his or her own shadow, as happens with a ceiling light.

The Kitchen 75

104

104 When its folding doors are closed, this kitchen, with its uniform white fronts, looks like a laboratory. With the doors open, however, one feels that it is indeed a kitchen, no matter how unconventionally laid out.

The large unit in the center combines in a minimum of space the stove, sink, breakfast table, dishwasher, floor cabinets, and a wooden butcher-block counter that permits the cook to sit down while at work. The stove at the back of the sink is equipped with a rigid gooseneck faucet tall enough to permit filling even large pots without having to carry them around the unit from the sink. In this system the walls are left free for built-in cabinets. On the stove side, there is a place for everything needed for cooking: pots, pans, food supplies, canned goods, as well as a good-sized compartment for cookbooks and a telephone. On the sink side, there is a place for glasses, tableware, drinks, and a bar shelf.

If the kitchen opens directly into other rooms, special care should be taken with its decoration. Too sterile a kitchen can make the adjoining areas seem cold and businesslike. When the open plan makes compromises necessary, preference should be given to the aesthetic aspect, whereas in separate rooms nothing prevents the practical side from getting its due. Yet the great advantage of the open kitchen is that the cook need never feel, or be, out of things.

76 The Kitchen

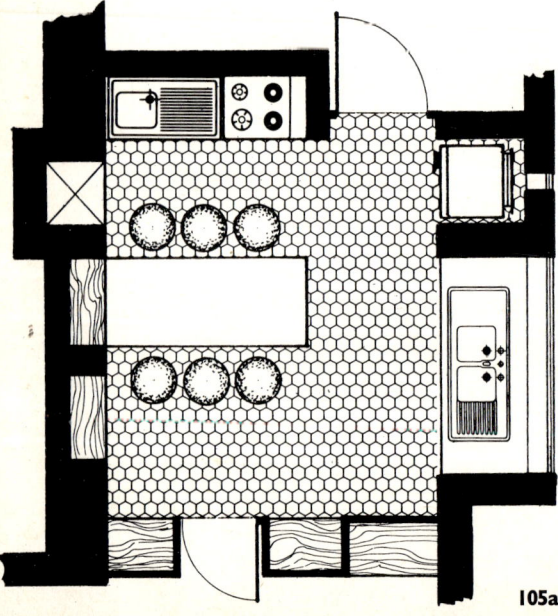

105

105, 106 Relatively small as this kitchen in a Danish one-family house is, it is made to seem much more spacious and interesting by its vaulted ceiling and the mirror-backed wall niches, which give rise to quite unexpected views. The basic black and white of the room create an appropriate setting for the varying combinations of kitchen utensils and supplies. In the stove niche, copper pans and kitchen knives make a rustic arrangement in which even a string of garlic plays its part. The oven is built into the wall near the burner top. The three mirrored niches take care of everything needed at mealtimes: coffee service, pepper grinder, mustard and marmalade jars, even the apéritifs— all at hand directly above the dining table.

105a

78   The Kitchen

107   A small, simply furnished kitchen and dining area in which equipment and design cooperate in creating a serene atmosphere. Household necessities, glassware, and utensils are neatly arranged on open shelves, a solution which strikes one as a refreshing relief from overplanning. Behind the work counter, the wall is covered with natural wood boards; these are also used for the dining table. The narrow shelf above the stove and sink is decidedly practical, affording place for permanently fixed objects such as a kitchen clock, electric plugs, a coffee grinder, and an electric can opener.

The Kitchen 79

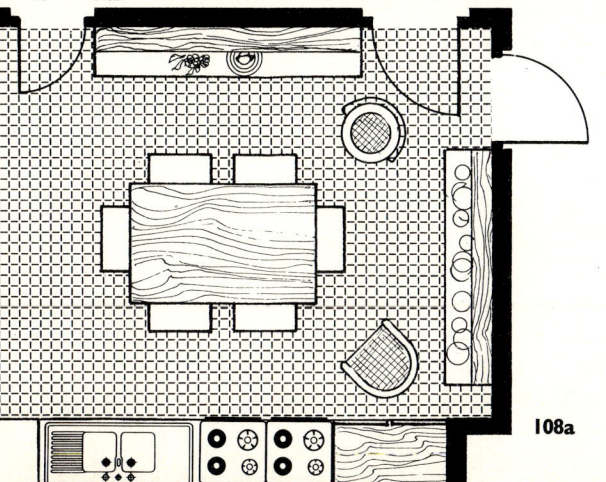

108

108a

108 The British designer Terence Conran designed the kitchen in his London house in farmhouse style. The Victorian chairs, the large dining table in the center, the built-in dresser against the rear wall with its simple forms and open display of pots and containers—all strike a country note, less through the materials used than because of the way they are arranged. Only the ceiling spots trained on the dining area and the lights concealed on the underside of the open-shelf cabinet on the left remind us that this is a modern kitchen.

The Kitchen

109, 110   A full bank of shelves between two windows divides this medium-sized kitchen into a playroom for the small children (plate 109) and a compactly arranged L-shaped cooking and work area (plate 110). One side of the shelf unit is open to the children's room and takes care of their playthings, while the other half, opening on the kitchen, holds kitchen equipment and supplies. A simple folding gate prevents the youngsters from entering the kitchen on their own (at least until they learn to open it).

The Kitchen

111

112

111, 112 With great ingenuity, the entire kitchen here was spanned by a framework of shining blue steel tubing with long hooks on which everything imaginable can be hung—from food supplies and utensils to a children's swing—a solution as practical as it is original, with everything necessary within comfortable reach of grownup hands yet out of reach of small meddlers. The red floor covering, the ceiling painted yellow down to the height of the tubular framework, the brightcolored cabinet fronts, and the bold geometrical pattern of the tabletop create a color scheme as unconventional and exciting as the steel construction it goes with.

THE BEDROOM
CHILDREN'S ROOMS
THE TEENAGER'S ROOM
STUDIES AND HOBBY ROOMS

The Bedroom

113 To make for greater seclusion, this bedroom has no window but only narrow vertical strips of glass, which provide all the light needed. Two closets were built on the outside wall; separating them by the window strips gives them a lighter effect than would a continuous front. Two transparent acrylic armchairs and a small round table are arranged into an intimate conversation group. The bright, warm mood of the room owes much to the use of yellow and orange as the only colors set against the white of the walls and ceiling, except for the large wall hanging, with its strong color accent.

114 A simple but very carefully furnished small bedroom in a house in the country. Raw wood and exposed beams lend the room a homey note to which the clear forms and strong colors of modern pictures and posters make an effective contrast. Considerable space is left between the beds, making the room appear more spacious and open than would a conventional plan with a double bed or closely juxtaposed twin beds in the middle.

86 The Bedroom

115

115 Large, uncluttered walls help make this small bedroom seem spacious even though there is scarcely room for more than the bed. A row of low boxlike units provides drawers and cabinets of various sizes. The quiet tones of the floor covering, bedspread, and cushions are nicely coordinated and lend the room a tasteful atmosphere heightened by the colors of the pictures and flowers.

116, 117 This bright, open bedroom in an American house is furnished with exquisite simplicity. An elegant tubular steel chair by Mies van der Rohe is juxtaposed to an early American wardrobe. The large picture window looking directly onto the terrace offers a fine view. A second, much smaller window above the beds can be closed off with folding wooden shutters. The fireplace is raised off the ground in a rough stone pilaster, so that even in bed one can watch the flames.

116

The Bedroom 87

88 The Bedroom

118

119

118   This small, high-ceilinged room was made to look larger by means of two tall mirrors. Two basic colors were used—a creamy white for the walls and a strong blue for the built-in shelf units. These colors are repeated in the spread and the headboard of the bed, the checkerboard pattern of which dominates everything and creates a clear spatial effect that helps compensate for the smallness of the room.

120   A bedroom directly under the eaves, furnished simply and discreetly. Though daylight enters only through small skylights and a narrow window near the bed, the room, with its large white surfaces, is bright and friendly. A narrow shelf behind the bed must suffice as night table, since freestanding tables would have required too much room and blocked access to the closet, an arrangement which takes advantage of the space under the sloping roof. The sliding doors of the wardrobes do not project into the room. The flexible lamps can be turned one way for reading in bed, the other for lighting the picture on the wall.

119   The dark-colored floor, walls, and ceiling transform this room into a cave for sleeping, an effect that is intensified by the lavish fur bedspread. Only the pictures looming dramatically out of the dark background mitigate the sense of being snugly away from it all.

90 The Bedroom

121

122

121 A snug and thoughtfully furnished bedroom separated from the living room by an open bookcase. The low shelf along the walls serves as night table, generally handy surface, and base for the flat cushions of a couch. The television set is fastened to the ceiling by a long rod and can be swiveled around. Yellow walls make the room seem light and spacious.

122 This bedroom could be mistaken for a living room. Two beds with toss pillows and a chaise-longue are arranged to make a seating group, and certainly the checkerboard-patterned bedspreads are not what is usually thought of as "bedroomy." The two little tables, stacked one above the other during the day, come apart to make separate night tables. The dark-brown walls promote a feeling of seclusion, especially at night with the curtains drawn, while during the day they provide a deliberate foil for the great sweep of landscape beyond the windows.

The Bedroom 91

123

123 A uniform facing of natural wood makes this room seem a truly secluded retreat. To avoid disturbing the restful atmosphere, neutral grays were used for the floor covering and bedspread, the only color accent being the bright orange-and-red throw laid across the foot of the bed.

92   The Bedroom

124

124   With a dash of the unconventional, a bedroom can be made to serve as a studio during the day. Originally the beds in this room stood conventionally side by side in the middle, with a night table on either side. When the room was redesigned, they were moved to the left and right of the window ledge, which was widened to make a dressing table and to conceal the radiator. During the day, blankets and pillows are kept out of sight in the large chest in the right foreground, and the beds become two comfortable sofas backed by round bolsters covered with the same material as is used for the bed and curtains. Opposite the bed-sofas is a pleasant place to work, with a small writing table and a handy shelf along the wall.

125 A further step was taken when this narrow bedroom was redesigned as a second living room. The beds were placed at right angles to make a pleasant seating group. The low partition serves as night table, chests for the bedding and other storage, and writing table. Stationery and the like are kept in a cabinet on casters that rolls under the writing ledge. Unfortunately, because of shortage of space, the bookcase had to be put behind the farthest bed, where it is difficult to get to.

125

126, 127 This feminine bedroom is furnished with loving care. Despite the numerous pictures and tiny art objects, its lightness and the open area in the center make the room look spacious and uncluttered. Writing materials and memorandum books are kept in an open file cabinet, to which a small and graceful three-tiered end table makes an attractive companion piece.

The Bedroom

128

129

128, 129 A studio was devised here. The ocher-brown walls, dark-green carpet, and matchboard sloping ceiling over the living area of this studio give the entire room an intimate atmosphere. The sleeping area is sparsely furnished, with only a bed, a headboard-shelf behind it, and a chest. In the study, a large L-shaped desk was set up, along with a reference library and a corner to sit in. The color of the sofa blends with that of the walls, while the finish of the desk and bookcases matches that of the very fine old chair. With its numerous accessories, books, and pictures, the study is more casual than the sleeping area. Two separate rooms could easily have been made here, but at the cost of openness and a pleasant interplay between the two zones.

The Bedroom

130

131

130 A floor-to-ceiling mirror makes this bedroom appear broad and open. The ceiling is slightly lower above the bed, and—together with the dark walls—gives the impression of an alcove clearly set off from the remainder of the room. The colors of the toss pillows echo the painting on the wall. In the mirror, the dressing table in front of the window can be seen.

131 This is a calm and well-balanced bedroom, thanks to the harmony between the black bedspread, against which the vicuna throw stands out splendidly, the black upholstery of the armchairs with their bright yellow and red pillows, and the dark-brown carpeting.

132 The seating group and bed here take up ▶ almost equal space, but the sleeping area is furnished much more quietly, with only the Andy Warhol serigraph of Elizabeth Taylor to enliven it. The conversation corner, with its red easy chairs and solid cube table, stands out much more, and, along with the powerfully composed painting by Nicholas Krushenick, dominates the room.

The Bedroom

132

133

133 This bedroom on the upper floor of a house owes a good deal of its attractiveness to a happy blend of architecture and furniture. The matchboard ceiling spans the room like a tent and gives it breadth but also, thanks to its warm texture, makes it cozy. There is only a low wall behind the head of the bed, and the ceiling continues beyond this wall to project over the living room on the floor below. The result is a strong feeling of depth, furthered by the indirect lighting and the linear sweep of the narrow ceiling boards. The unobtrusive furniture also adds to the spaciousness of the room. Instead of night tables, open compartments were built into the wall behind the bed; the light armchair on the left and the wide, low bed are the only pieces of freestanding furniture. The restrained brown and beige of the bedspread and carpet give the finishing touch to an atmosphere of dignity and restraint.

134, 135 Quite unlike the previous example, everything here is based on decided contrasts. The white rug under the writing table, the white chair, and the white bedspread stand out sharply against the dark carpeting. Stimulating, too, are the very different materials and textures used for the walls and ceiling. A grasscloth-covered wall is behind the bed, the walls leading to the bathroom and living room are painted white, the ceiling is matchboard, and a large bank of windows extends across the whole width of the room. A net curtain unemphatically marks off the rear of the bedroom, with its dressing table and built-in closet.

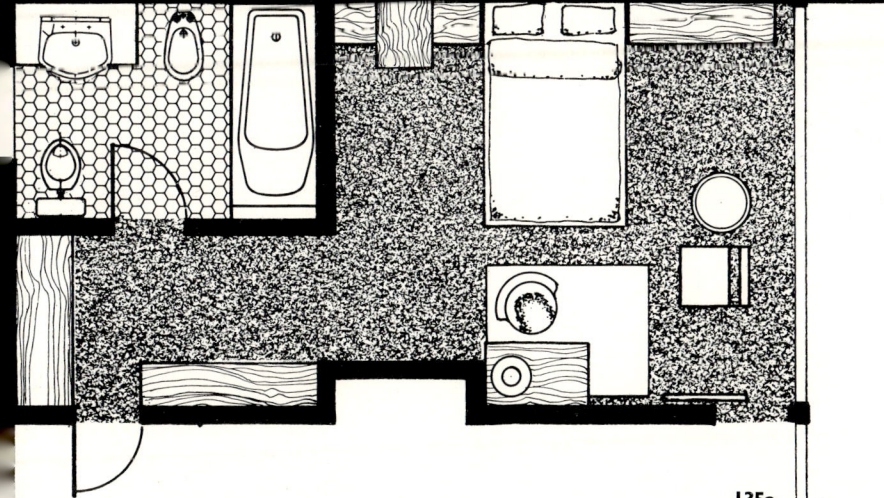

134

135

135a

Children's Rooms 101

137

◀ 136 This room is so small that it can scarcely hold more than the triple-bunk bed. At the head of each bunk there are shelves on which each child can store his own toys, books, stuffed animals, and the like, and each bunk has its own small wall lamp. This solution neatly replaces the need for separate rooms, at least through the early school years.

137 It is sensible to set up a child's room at the start in such a way that, as he grows, the necessary adjustments and modifications can be made without undue effort or expense. Although the crib will eventually have to be exchanged for a normal bed, the furniture seen here, with its many open shelves for toys and its drawers with slots large enough for growing hands to grip, will serve the child well through several more years.

Children's Rooms

It is not easy to find the right bed for a child's room. Not only is the age of the child a prime factor, but the dimensions of the room, suitable or otherwise, must be taken into account. A crib is perfect for an infant—he can look out, be looked at, be kitchy-kooed, and not fall out—but it is soon outgrown. When that happens, unless space is limited, nothing prevents one from buying a full-size bed that will serve right through the teens. If two or more children share the room, bunk beds leave more floor space free for playing. By building them in or setting them up on a solid frame, as many as three bunks can be superimposed (plate 136). Setting them as shown in plate 140 gives the child in the lower bed more freedom of movement.

138 Closets and beds are combined here. The red wooden construction serves as both ladder and guard rails and, together with the red drawers for toys under the lower bed, strikes a bright and cheerful note. A worktable with places for two is placed beneath the window.

139 No fewer than four children are provided for here in two robust doubledecker bunks. The furniture is designed for both practical use and play. The plastic chairs can be stacked, and the various-sized red plastic shelf units are so light that even small children can handle them.

Children's Rooms

140 A two-bed room furnished with originality and at small expense. Wooden shelves run the length of the wall and function as underpinning for the mattresses and as a table too; beneath them are storage units for bedding and toys. The simple composition of furniture in dark pine and the glowing colors of the coverlets and pillows go very well in the rustic atmosphere of beamed ceiling, brick tile flooring, and rough, whitewashed walls.

141 Combining bed, chest of drawers, and shelves for books and playthings into a single freestanding island in the middle of the room makes an arrangement almost certainly more appealing to a child than the conventional plan and also allows additional space for play.

Schoolchildren need a good place to work in, but they should also have a table for games, painting, and puttering. It should have as good lighting and as generous a work surface as any adult's desk or writing table. To encourage good posture, the chair must be easily movable and should make it possible for the child to sit comfortably and correctly at his table. With more than one youngster in the room, each should have a workplace of his own, to be arranged and kept as best suits him. Even if the room is small, a proper table and two chairs can always be set up in front of a window (plate 138).

104 Children's rooms

142

143

142, 143 This ensemble can be used for many years. The baby bed (plate 143) is no more than a frame with low side walls for protection. Diapers and other baby things can be stored in the shallow chest at the end of the bed. In later years, if one removes the sides and adds cushions, the bed becomes a comfortable bench to lie or sit on while playing or reading (plate 142). The chest is now used to store playthings, and the chest of drawers—formerly used for diaper-changing—can serve as a low table for painting by the attaching of a panel to the second drawer.

Children's rooms 105

144

145

144, 145 A permanent wooden framework, firmly fixed and child-resistant, was built within this room as an aid in making alterations as the child grows. The baby's cradle can be hung by ropes from the construction (plate 144), to be replaced later by a regular bed (plate 145). With rods, rungs, and canvas mats slung at various levels, the construction then becomes ideal for climbing and other healthy exercise. The wall on the left is lined with drawers, cabinets, and open shelves.

Children's Rooms

146 Here a recess in a storage wall accommodates a large desk which, being on rollers, can be moved to a window overlooking a terrace. With its ample drawer and storage space on either side, the desk can serve well right through the child's teens.

147 A two-boy room where each has his own workplace. The writing table of the younger boy was placed at right angles to a row of cabinets the front of which was covered with a special paint to make them serve as a blackboard. The tables of light natural wood are of simple and robust construction; their white Formica tops can be raised or lowered as needed.

148   In this model workplace, the table and chair can be moved about as desired. The table, with its Formica top, can be tilted without effort so that the child need not lean across it. Directly above the table there is space on the wall to pin up school schedules, pictures, and notes. Additional work surface and shelf space are afforded by a second table in front of the window and by the red shelves for books and playthings. Proof, in short, that even the narrowest space can be furnished for a child's comfort.

108 Children's Rooms

149

150

151

152

Here are four original, inexpensive, and easy ideas to utilize in almost any child's room.

149 The carpet design makes a giant game board and gives the room freshness and originality.

150 A large recess in the shelf wall serves as clothes closet, play area, and bench; it is painted to match the oilcloth on the round play table, a table low enough for children to squat around comfortably on flat cushions laid on the floor.

151 Painted cardboard furniture is far sturdier than anxious parents might imagine. Lightweight and easily moved around, it is also inexpensive enough to be replaced whenever needed or desired.

152 Since the space above a single bed is generally left unused, here two ladders were combined to make an ideal apparatus for climbing and gymnastics, and the bed is there to break any falls. The canvas sling, hung from above, makes a fine hideout.

Children's Rooms 109

153 Two metal shelf constructions divide this room into a sleeping area with two beds, a workplace at the window, and a place to play in. The constructions are so firmly fixed that young apes and Tarzans can swing from them or clamber up them to get at the top shelves. The worktable in the middle of the room can be folded up to clear space for one large play area. Books and playthings on the open shelves add their note of liveliness.

110 Children's Rooms

154

155

154–56 Here we have a fine split-level playroom. On a balcony built into the corner above the bed (plate 156) the children can sit around a small table and play their games. Playthings are kept on the gallery in red-painted shelves opened up in the floor-to-ceiling storage wall (plate 155). A board pierced with large circles makes a ladder leading up to the platform. Under the bed are drawers for toys; the drawers also have large wheels and long pull rods, and thus can be used as wagons. The second bed, on the opposite wall (plate 154), is a Murphy-type construction which folds into the wall during the day. A large bookcase, subject to all sorts of variations, was constructed of wooden boxes, cubes with drawers, and red shelves. In the middle of the room a climbing pole with double-sided rungs rises all the way to the ceiling. Painting the storage wall in two colors made the room appear broader (plate 155).

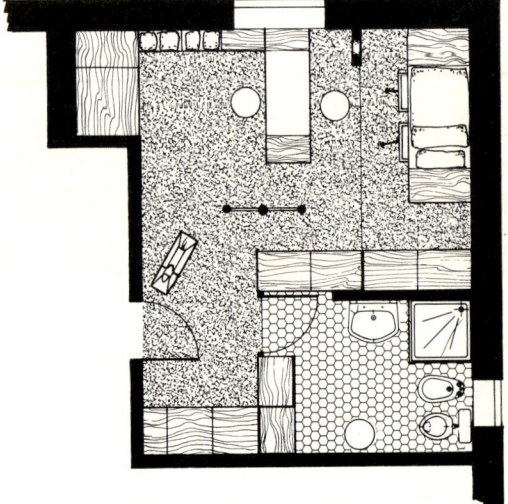

155a

156 ▶

Children's Rooms

157

158

159

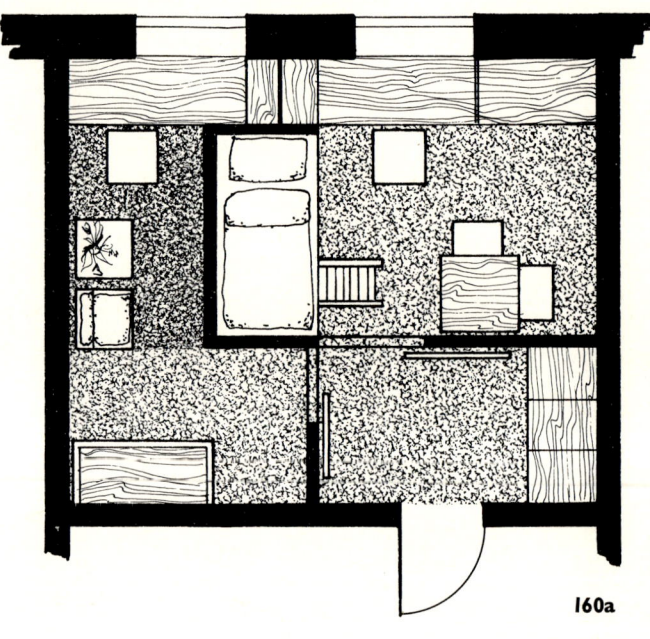

160a

157–60 If the children's room has more than one window, it can easily be converted into two rooms by a simple divider wall. Here, however, two good-sized single rooms were made out of one by a really ingenious expedient. Two beds are superimposed like double-decker bunks in the middle of the room (plate 160), but a partition separates the lower bed from the boy's room, and the upper bed is similarly screened off from the girl's room. The result is two separate sleeping compartments which, together, take up no more space than a single

Children's Rooms 113

160

bed. The rest of the room can be divided off by the white sliding doors.

In the boy's room (plate 158), the basic color is a strong yellow which returns in various tones on almost every item of furnishing. The worktable in front of the window continues into the other "room," broken only by a double-sided bookcase. The ledge above the window is handy for storing things but also corrects the proportions of the room which, as a result of having been divided in two, is really too high for its width. A chest (out of the children's old room) and a play table with three simple stools complete the furnishings.

The girl's room (plate 157) is done in red and shocking pink. The wooden armchair and its matching table are brought close to the bed to make a small sitting room during the day. An old wardrobe was painted white and its center panel was decorated with the same material used for the shades (plate 159).

The Teenager's Room

161 Overcrowded and a little off-beat like so many young people's rooms nowadays, there is no unified style or carefully worked-out arrangement of furniture and pictures here, but who can deny that the room has warmth, sociability, and unmistakable individuality?

The Teenager's Room

162, 163 A cozy room arranged in an improvised and very personal manner which is not too restless, even with all its colorfulness. The green of the walls and ceilings reflects the green of the trees in the garden. A narrow part of the room (plate 162) was covered with a pegboard panel where photos and posters can be displayed, and belts and other accessories can be hung from hooks without damaging the wall. Alongside the table (plate 163) there is room for a record player and tape recorder on a low shelf unit.

162
163

The Teenager's Room

164   This teenager's room in a Milan home was set up simply and unpretentiously but with a good deal of thought. Although the window is of normal size, the light curtain and the open bookshelves at either side of the opening give the illusion of a picture window extending from floor to ceiling. In front of it stands an ingenious folding table which is easily removed if there is a horde of visitors. The walls are left bare to keep the room from seeming too narrow. A rug protects what is left of an already well-battered parquet floor.

165   The bed and two easy chairs are covered with the same fabric and make a seating group. In this poorly lighted attic room, the dormer windowsill was widened to make a worktable, a not very successful solution, since the writing surface is still too limited.

The Teenager's Room   117

166

167

166, 167 An irregular ceiling, sloping in several directions, sets the character of this attic room. Nooks and recesses have been cleverly exploited with continuous built-in elements. The bed (plate 167) rests on a long platform which serves also as a place to store things and has drawers for the bedding. During the day, wedge bolsters at the back convert it into a comfortable sofa. The iron stove (plate 166) is more than a conversation piece; though the room has central heating, the stove is often used when friends gather on a chilly evening.

118 The Teenager's Room

168

170

169

168–70 These are the rooms of a brother and sister, and although each has similar furnishings, the different color schemes create quite different atmospheres. White walls and strong colors make the boy's room (plate 168) unfussy and direct, an impression also borne out by the shelves supported by brackets on exposed metal strips. At the foot of the bed, the wall system supports a long low cabinet unit which holds the audio components and also serves as night table, and one side of the large writing table is attached to one of the horizontal braces of the wall system. With its flowered wallpaper and blue curtains and carpeting, the girl's room (plates 169, 170) strikes a softer, frillier note. Here the worktable, bookcase, dressing table, and chest of drawers form a unit along the window wall. The two white armchairs and the small round table can be drawn up around the bed to make a seating group.

Studies and Hobby Rooms

171

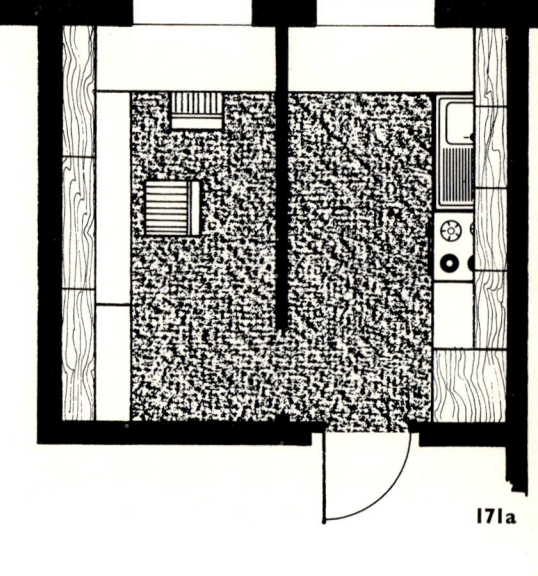

171a

171 A simple partition can separate a household utility room from a large kitchen. All the basic equipment is nicely fitted into the space available. A wide L-shaped ledge is adequate for writing or sewing and gets good light from the extension lamps above it. Books, file boxes with recipes, darning materials, sewing basket—all have their place on two shelves above the ledge, and there are two chests, for shoes and laundry, which can be rolled out of sight under the ledge. A sturdy sisal carpet covers the cold kitchen tiles. Practical as the room may be in function and furnishing, the aesthetic side was not neglected. The white partition is graphically broken up by black molding, making a contrast repeated in the white worktable and black chairs, shelves, and lamps.

172

172 A wall of built-in units can accommodate in a minimum of space everything needed for housework—shelves either open or concealed behind doors, a cupboard for the iron, a fold-down ironing board, a swivel-mounted sewing machine. This combination of utilities fits into almost any space and can supplement, though not entirely replace, a separate room for housework. In any case, clearly arranged and practically organized, such a unit does much to make housekeeping easier and more efficient.

Studies and Hobby Rooms 121

173 Lighting is often a problem in attic workrooms, since generally the windows are small and few. To compensate here, the entire room was painted white and a light-colored wooden floor was laid to get the most out of whatever daylight does get past the low-sloping eaves. The metal shelf construction set across the room marks off two separate workplaces.

122 Studies and Hobby Rooms

174

175

174 Casually furnished as it may be, this is a well-arranged workroom. The trestle table in the middle of the room gets direct daylight through the large window and artificial light from the two hanging lamps fastened to the wall. If needed, additional lights can be attached to a metal track along the wall. Plans, papers, and the like are stored in a movable file cabinet.

175 Bright-yellow étagères and chairs lend warmth and life to this simply furnished study. Because the room is small, the table is set flush against the wall between the two étagères, which also serve to support one end of the table.

Studies and Hobby Rooms

176 By clever division of space, this not particularly large room was made into a highly versatile study and hobby room. A scaffolding of painted blue-green supports the tables and the bed. A drafting table is placed crosswise in the foreground, and there is a large worktable along the wall. A board with nails and hooks keeps tools within easy reach. Wire baskets under the table serve as drawers. The netting stretched over the scaffolding can be reached by the ladder on the left and used as an unconventional hammock. A large cloth mat with sewn-on pockets holds magazines. The white arrows on the black-painted floor are traffic signs which serve as a warning against catching one's feet on the low crossbar.

124 Studies and Hobby Rooms

177

178

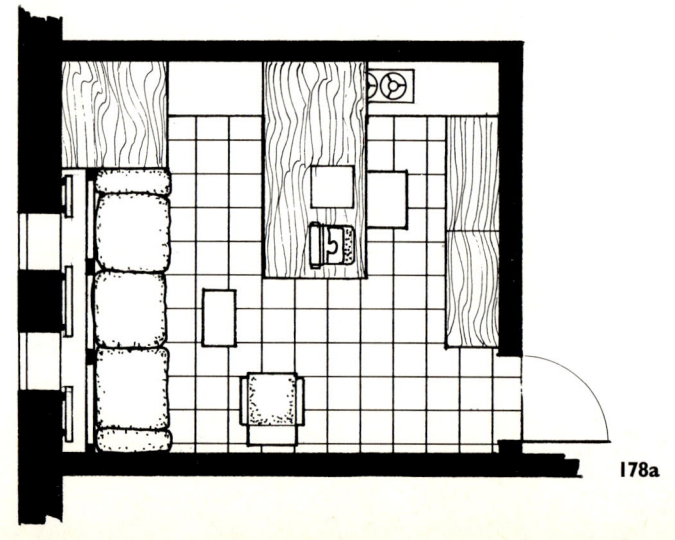
178a

Studies and Hobby Rooms

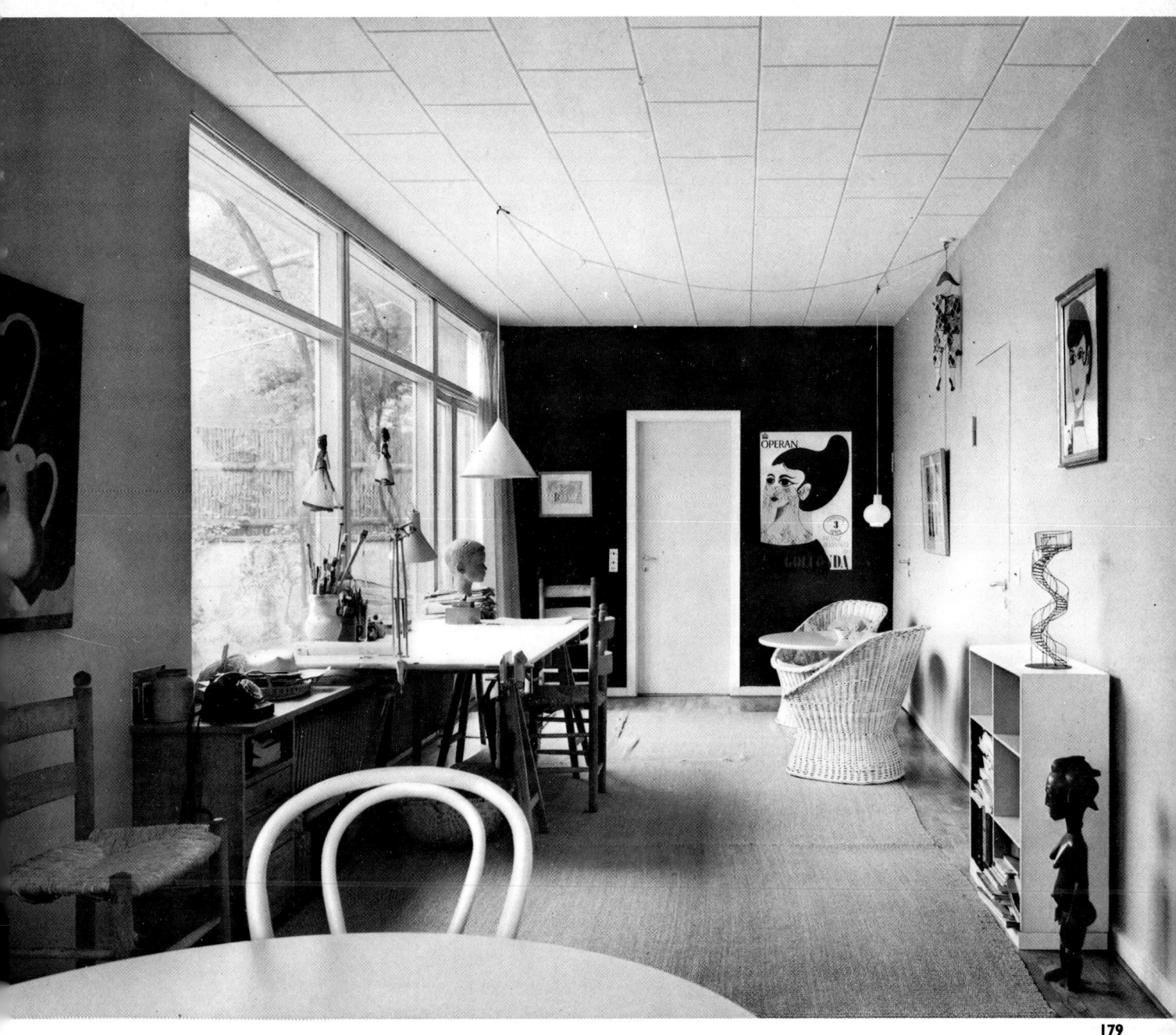

179

177, 178   Imagination and a gift for improvisation transformed this basement into a bright and cheerful study. Since the only daylight filtered in wanly through two high windows opening on air shafts, powerful fluorescent tubes were fixed to the wall and then masked by large panes of frosted glass to give the illusion of natural light (plate 177). To enhance this effect, the entire room was kept white. With stone and cement walls and floor, it was hard to keep the heat in and the cold out, so the floor was covered with several layers of insulating material and the walls with sheets of fiberboard which, incidentally, make an excellent surface for pinning up notes and photos. Egg cartons were used to insulate the ceiling and improve the acoustics. Comparable ingenuity was lavished on the furnishings. The large writing table consists of a panel which rests on A-frames on one end and, on the other, is attached to a molding along the wall so it can be removed when necessary. The two hanging lamps are on tracks and can be adjusted to the position of the table. They also light the bench, coffee table, and lightweight easy chair at the blind window, creating a pleasant corner for listening to music or reading. Storage space is provided by a deep corner bookcase accessible from two sides and by a wall ledge with drawers beneath it.

179   In this Danish house, a room which was really only a hallway leading to other rooms was converted into a studio and dining room. The entrance doors are set flush into the wall and are unobtrusive, but there is little wall space between them. The large working and drafting table was given the choice place directly in front of the window, and the radiator was covered by a wide ledge that continues across the window to provide additional shelving. At the left, the ledge rests on a small cabinet holding drawing supplies and other accessories.

180

181

A library is more than a place to store books. It should be a room to which one can retire at ease with everything at hand—comfortable armchair, a place for ashtray and glasses, a small writing table or, depending on the sort of thing one does, a good-size desk, plus whatever special furniture or equipment is required for one's profession or interests.

180 This library was furnished with a few choice pieces. The overall warm brown tone goes well with the metal étagère and makes for a peaceful atmosphere.

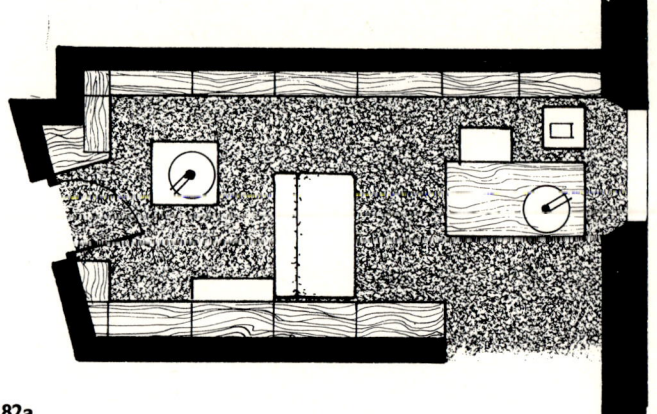

182a

181 To keep this rather narrow room as open as possible, shelves and table were fitted into an alcove and a glass-topped brass table was used. The shelves are also edged in brass. A file cabinet was built into a section of the bookcase wall. The room seems highly personal, relaxed, and sympathetic, partly because the shelves and furnishings are of fine quality and yet no fuss was made about setting the books in any rigid order.

182 The white shelves, door, and furniture make a quiet setting for the books, and allow the red sofa to stand out strikingly. The radio and phonograph are deftly concealed on the lower rear shelves to the right of the door. The small chest is on casters and can be moved anywhere in the room to serve all sorts of purposes. What space was available was exploited with ingenuity, as witness the drawers built into the door recess beyond the rear bookcase wall.

Studies and Hobby Rooms

183

184
185

183–86 A single room with no end of functions —gym, household room, studio, guest room, storeroom—all in an attic! Under the sloping windows are two workplaces with a common tabletop supported on a chest and an open shelf unit. The gym and play area (used also for drying clothes indoors) includes wall bars, climbing ropes, and a swing (plates 184, 185). The guest bed in the alcove by the head of the stairs is flanked by a bookcase. On the wall opposite the workplaces there are shelves for equipment, hobby material, and magazines (plate 185)—these can be concealed with match-stick blinds. Strong colors, the light wood floors, and built-in elements give the room an airy and inviting look. In short, a good example of what can be done with a minimum of expense and a maximum of imagination to convert an unused room into a place enjoyed by the entire family.

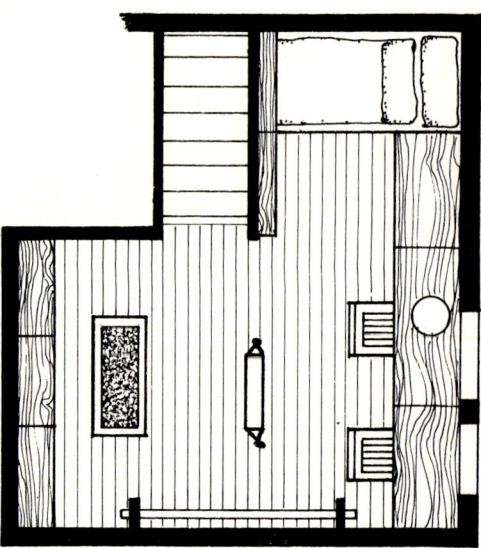

186a

THE HOUSE AS A WHOLE

132 The House as a Whole

187

188

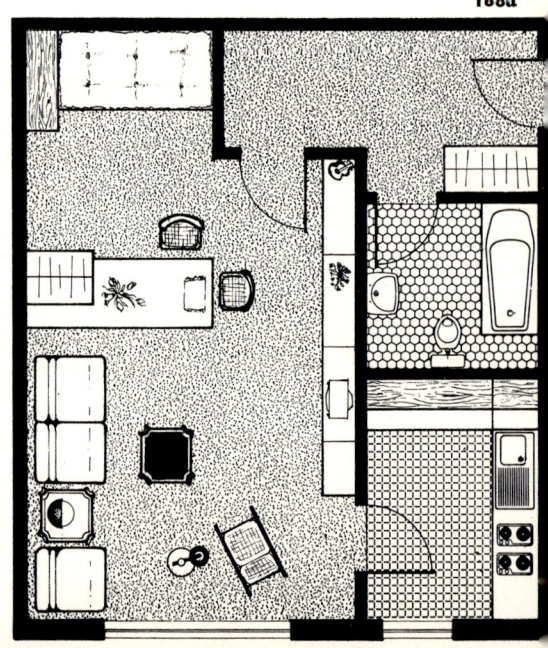

188a

The House as a Whole 133

189

190

191

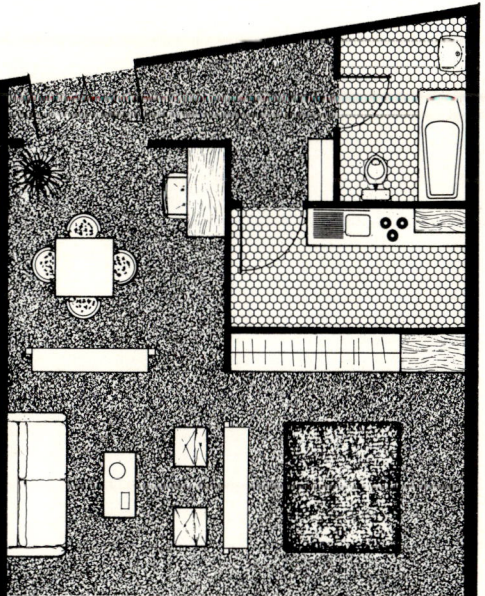

191a

187, 188   In this small room, the back of an old wardrobe was encased within a built-in unit disguised as an engaged structural pier. The unit acts as a divider between the living and sleeping areas. Shelves and a large table, used for both eating and working, make a multipurpose piece of furniture combining quite different functions in little space. A row of low cabinets along one wall is used for storage, as a sideboard during meals, and as a base for the television set. The vinyl-covered chairs and the small tables are easily rearranged into a seating group. Yellow was chosen for the walls and carpet to make the room appear wider, but in the long run so bright a color may prove to be a little hard to live with.

189–91   Exquisite modern furnishings make this Parisian one-room apartment something special. In the L-shaped room, white metal shelves suffice to mark the dining and work area off from the living and sleeping area. The distance between shelves was deliberately made high in order to minimize visual interruption in the room. The bright tapestry on the back wall of the sleeping area (plate 190) is equally effective viewed from the living area (plate 189). To keep the sleeping quarters with their large double bed from seeming too obtrusive, the bedspread and the floor covering are of similar quiet grays. All in all, a very bright and open apartment, in which the nicely balanced arrangement of the furniture plays a considerable part.

192

192–94 An ideal small open-plan apartment in which the separate zones are each conceived quite differently but combine to make an exciting whole. The individual sectors are easily closed off by accordion partitions (whose dark wood does, however, look rather heavy when they are closed). Even the kitchen (plate 192) is incorporated into the main room, its bright colors contrasting with the restful mood of the living area. The shelves with their row of small red drawers and the matching red cookware set against a white background look lighter and more decorative than would standard closed hanging cabinets. The kitchen and living-room area (plate 193) are separated by a large dining and worktable which is nothing more than a flush door painted yellow and set on simple trestles. In the sleeping area (plate 194), the conventional night table is replaced by three small stacked tables which can be used elsewhere as needed. A half-height cabinet separates the sleeping alcove from the immediately adjacent seating area and holds everything for which there is no room in the large closets in the entrance hall. While the pattern of the wallpaper is quite lively, its closely related colors tone down the overall effect.

The house as a whole   135

193

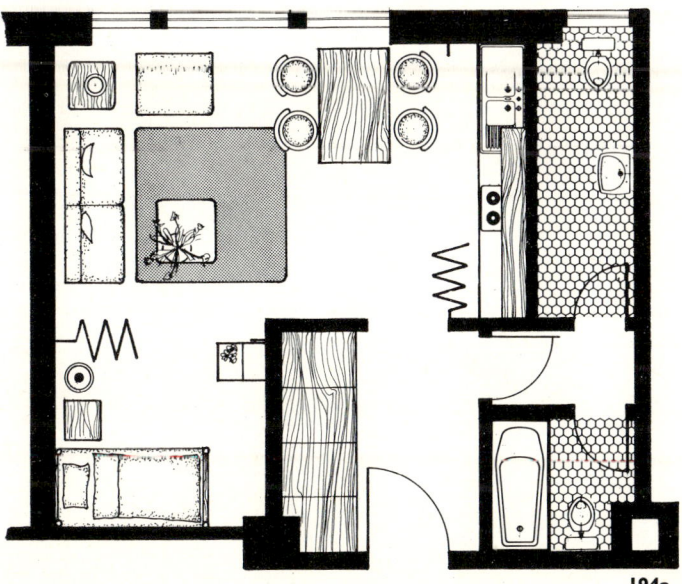

194

194a

195

196

197

198

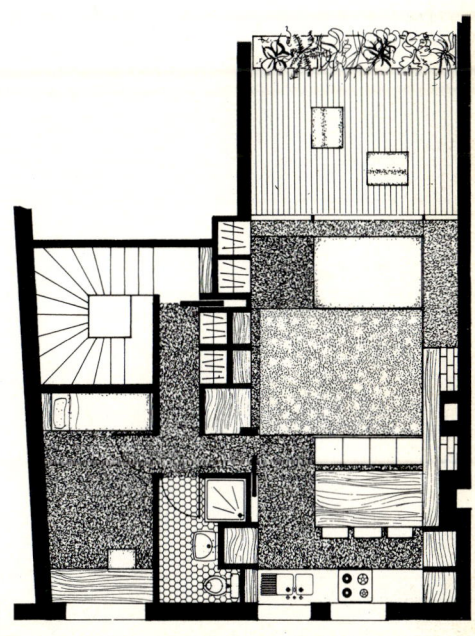
198a

195–98 A well worked-out division of space made it possible to comfortably accommodate a family with three children in a room whose total floor space is only slightly over 48 square yards. Besides a children's room, a narrow entrance hall with built-in closets, and the bathroom, there is an all-purpose room of average size and a terrace which was built on later to take advantage of the space beneath the low eaves, which could not easily be incorporated into the interior. On one end of the main room is the kitchen (plate 195), with its low windows completely surrounded by shelves. A ventilation hood prevents cooking smells from invading the living quarters. Evenings, the kitchen is shut off by a blind (plate 197) which looks just as if it covered a window. The cushioned bench of the dining table serves also as a sofa and combines with the bed and the fireplace (plate 196) to make up the seating group, which is further emphasized by the white carpet laid over the blue floor covering. Color is used discreetly, with white as the foundation. The texture of the rough-finished walls breaks up what would otherwise be an expanse of solid white. A few colored accessories and the blue carpeting enliven the room without crowding it, as bright colors would. This, together with the careful apportionment of areas, gives an impression of spaciousness.

138 The House as a Whole

199
200

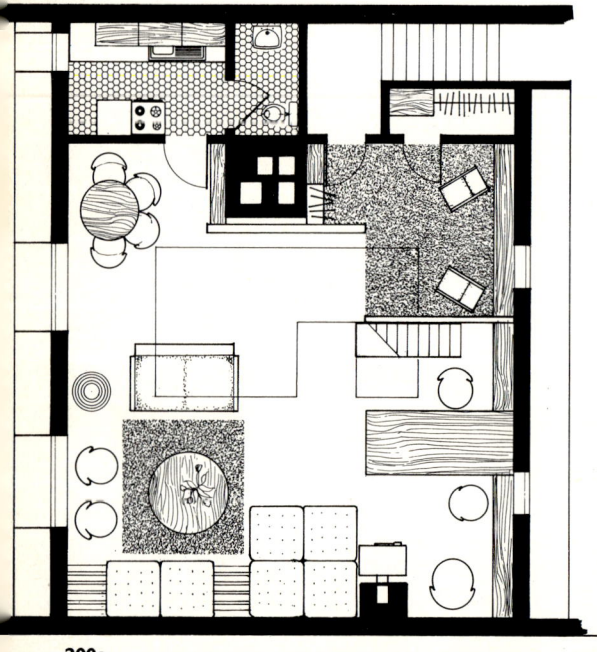

200a

The House as a Whole 139

201

199–201 The very tall attic of an eighteenth-century house in Copenhagen was divided into two levels and modernized; the modernization is most conspicuous in the new large windows and the open-floor plan. Only the shoring beams of the old attic, still visible here and there, testify to its age. In furnishing the apartment, the designer disregarded both unity and formality in favor of picking and choosing from different periods and styles.

The entrance is through a roomy foyer (plate 201) in which a nineteenth-century rocking chair immediately catches the eye. To the right, a thin divider screens off the workplace. The dining area in the alcove is marked off from the seating group by a sofa set crosswise (plate 199), but the two zones are subtly related in that the dining chairs and the armchairs have much the same shape. The front of the fireplace block was sheathed in copper, and its slightly reflecting surface makes the room appear larger.

Directly behind the dining area, but separate from it, lies the kitchen. The stylistic disparity between the simple benches, the elegant forms of the Arne Jacobsen furniture, and the patterned sofa gives real character to the unpretentious conversation group (plates 199, 200). Large white flat pillows set on bases of wooden slats make comfortable places to sit or sprawl, and are easily combined either to round off the conversation group or to serve as guest beds (plate 200). To give the living area a more enclosed feeling, the rear wall was painted brown. The larger part of the room is taken up by the studio, since the owner is a designer and works at home. The large worktable rests on a cabinet that houses a television set and bar (plate 201).

140 The House as a Whole

202

203

204

205

204a

205a

The House as a Whole 141

206

202–6 By distributing the basic activities of daily living over various levels, this small house contrives to accommodate five persons without their treading on each other's toes. Floors, walls, and ceilings in all of the rooms are covered in brown, against which the few white pieces of furniture stand out impressively. The entrance (plate 202) opens directly on the main room, which provides areas for dining, lounging, and sleeping. Not a square inch is wasted—the flat cushions on the stair of the lounging area can also serve as comfortable seats for the dining area; shelves running continuously along the wall not only conceal the radiators but also serve as a low side table for the seating group and as a serving table for the dining area. Behind the bank of tall wardrobes (plate 203) a stairway leads to the sleeping quarters on the upper level. A noteworthy detail is the use of blue light squares set into the floor; their diffuse light goes well with the unusual character of the room. In the other room there is sleeping space for three: on a lower level, two mattresses on platforms, and on an upper level, reached by a steep stair, a third bed. With all this, moreover, there is still room for a small study area.

142 The house as a whole

207

208

207–10 Gaily colored and easygoing are the words for this three-room apartment in which the disadvantages of a many-angled layout were superbly overcome. Compared with the other rooms, the living room (plates 207 and 210) is relatively discreet in its use of color. Its small space is further hemmed in by a built-in unit reaching almost to the ceiling; therefore excessive color contrast would only have made the room look even tighter. The relative sobriety of the room is, however, relieved by the use of brightly colored posters. The small dining area (plates 207, 209), with its white furniture, is not out of tune with the rest of the apartment, the folding chairs recalling garden furniture and

The house as a whole

209 210

therefore further stressing the informality of the room. The two freestanding open bookcases make a narrow passageway between the entrance and the living room, and also provide additional shelving for books without using up precious wall space. Toward the kitchen (plate 210, right), markedly stronger colors were used, with a glowing red setting the key. In the bedroom (plate 208) the neutral off-white background of the walls and curtains lends extra brilliance to the intense yellow, blue, and red which, though used sparingly, make the entire room very colorful. The large mirror helps make the narrow passage to the bedroom seem less cramped.

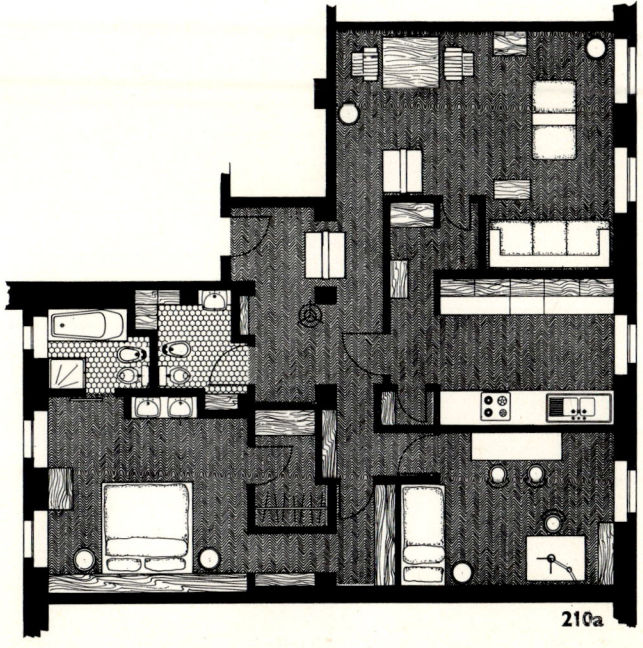

210a

144 The House as a Whole

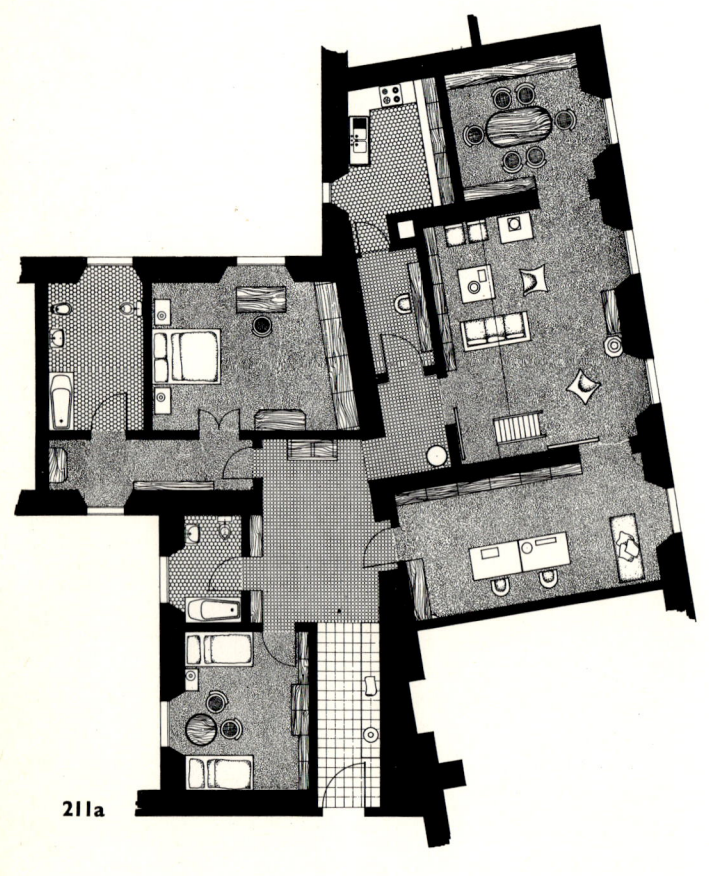

211a

211–14 In these rooms in an eighteenth-century Milan *palazzo*, only the vaulted ceiling still hints at the original style. With furnishings a seemingly casual mixture of old and new, an anti-style becomes a style of its own. Through the use of the same tiles for walls, floor, and bench, the long narrow entrance hall (plate 211) was made much more serene, especially in contrast with the heterogeneous furnishings of the other rooms. The living room, with its vaulted ceiling, was high enough to permit inserting a gallery (plates 213, 214). The safari chairs, the black metal bookcases, the old-fashioned coal-stove which, without its door, serves as a fireplace, and the inconspicuous, inexpensive, and hard-wearing gray fiber carpeting are all evidence of a casual style of living. The dining room (plate 214) is rather more stylistically unified and is pleasantly and diffusely illuminated by small black wall lamps that cast indirect light. In the studio, however (plate 212), there is once again a sympathetic air of planned improvisation. A long panel across the wall is used for continually changing combinations and arrangements of posters, photos, children's drawings, notes, and postcards; the wires from which industrial lamps are suspended have the functional simplicity of overhead cables.

214 ▶

211

212

213

The House as a Whole 145

215

216

217

The House as a Whole

215–19 This apartment was designed for a couple with two children and exploits various new ideas easily adaptable to the usual apartment dwelling. The children's room, master bedroom, bath, kitchen, dining area, and living room are laid out around two central alcoves. Within each alcove are trundle beds (plates 217, 218) which can be pulled into the room at night and extended to form double beds (plate 219). Built into the alcoves, and jutting out over the trundle beds when they are placed within the alcoves, are two wardrobe units with accordion doors painted to look like supergraphics (plates 217, 218). Strictly speaking, these are no longer rooms in the usual sense: washbasins, large worktables in front of windows, bookcases, wall ledges, light rattan chairs, and reading nooks in alcoves make the children's room and the master bedroom small dwellings within the dwelling. A unified and very graceful conception—in which there is even leeway for a bit of disorderliness—prevents one at first from realizing that these are genuinely separate rooms with different functions. What is outstanding here is that, besides the living room shared by all alike, each member of the family has a second living room to retire to, with furnishings that allow for a variety of activities. The ultimate advantage is that the entire family, individually and together, enjoys more recreational space than most apartments afford.

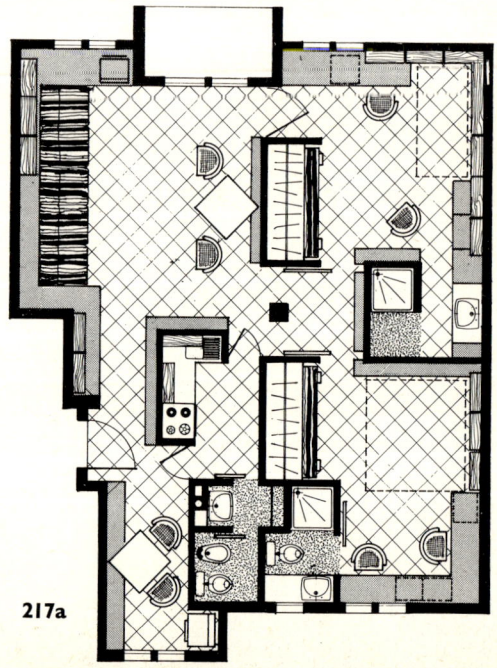

217a

218

219

148 The House as a Whole

220

221

222

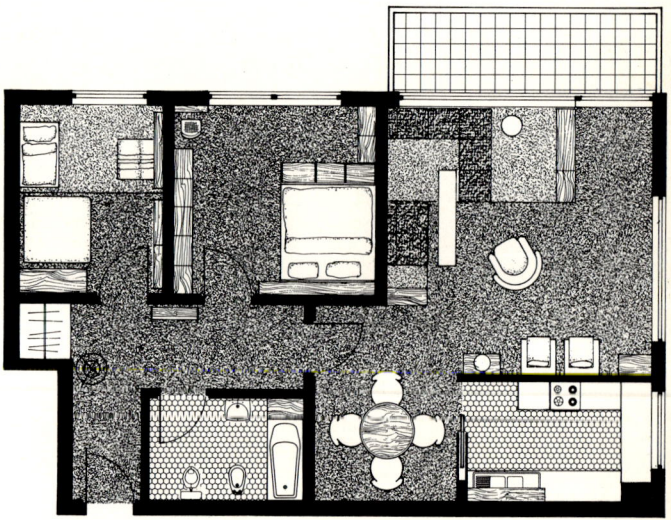

223a

220–23 Any apartment can be decorated in a contemporary and individualistic fashion without financial strain if a spirit of invention is wedded to a clever hand with tools, as this German three-room apartment with a quite standard floor plan shows. In the living room (plates 221, 223), a large platform was built in front of the window, and this accommodates armchairs, seating cushions, and a table designed to permit either formal

223

socializing or relaxed lounging. Warm brown tones in various shades balance the sober white of the furniture, and two floor-to-ceiling shelf units mark off the area from the rest of the room. In the bedroom (plate 220), another such shelf unit, painted red, was built by the owners, as was the platform. The shelf unit is close enough to the bed to leave room for a wardrobe behind it, and functions as night table and dressing table as well as holding books, accessories, and a television set. The effect is not that of a bedroom with a bookcase but that of a pleasant living room with a couch. The small room for the children (plate 222) was also broken up by a platform, with the bed and an armchair on the upper level, well out of the way of the play area on the lower level. A large drawer for toys makes good use of the space under the platform. Gaiety and color are introduced by the lively fabric of the curtains and the mattress pad which is used for playing on the floor.

224

225

226

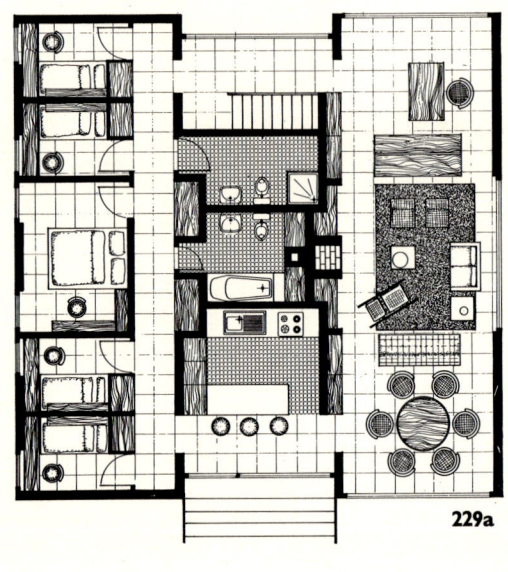

229a

227

228

224–29   What is especially striking in this house is how well everything was thought out. A square floor plan was divided into three parallel sectors of equal size. One of these contains the parents' bedroom (plate 227) and separate rooms for all four children; the central one contains the kitchen (plate 226), bath, and entrance hall; the third holds a large living room (plates 224, 225, 229) that stretches the entire length of the house, unbroken but with three zones clearly demarcated. On the ground floor, the overhang of the roof was exploited to make a covered play area for the children (plate 228) and a hobby room with large windows. The clear division of space is accompanied by unobtrusive contemporary furnishings that do not aim at unnecessary effect. Numerous built-in units—wall cabinets used as partitions between the children's rooms and the hall, alcoves with shelves around the kitchen and bath area, fixed components in the kitchen—made it possible to do without many freestanding elements. Should it prove desirable later, the wooden partitions between the children's rooms can easily be removed. Unobtrusive materials, such as wooden ceilings and slate floors, were used in all the rooms.

152 The House as a Whole

230

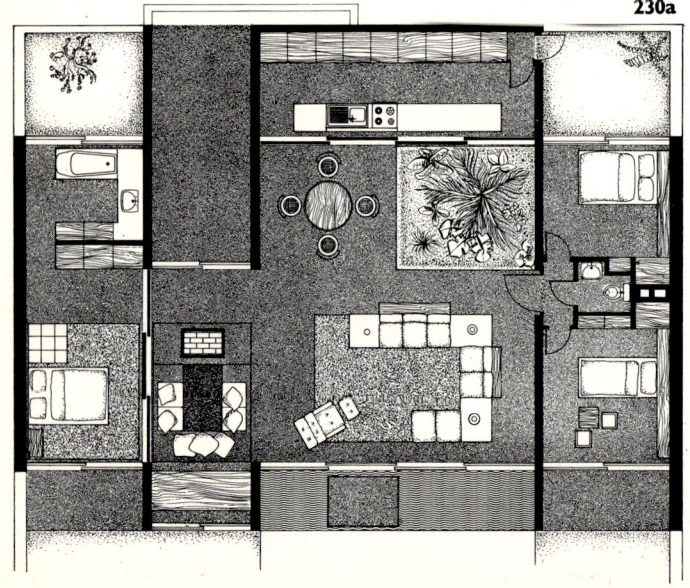

230a

230–32 In this house, which belongs to a French architect, structure and decoration, architecture and furnishings are closely attuned. The living room with dining area, bedroom, and kitchen is laid out on an open plan, but the separate areas can be closed off by beige sliding doors. The cushions of the seating group (plate 231) are laid on a long low platform which defines the area and also serves as tables and shelf surfaces. For more relaxed gatherings, around the fireplace there is a sunken lounging area with loose cushions (plate 230). In the kitchen, the work surfaces and stove stand free in the middle of the room like counters, so that while cooking one can look into the living room. White paneling screens off the stove. There are virtually no pictures or accessories because they would disturb the exciting interplay of large horizontal and vertical surfaces. Instead, this restful setting is enlivened by the rich vegetation of a winter garden.

The House as a Whole 153

231

232

154   The House as a Whole

233-38 Here wood, rough plaster, and brick strike just the right rustic note, countered by the uncompromising modernity of the overall style of furnishings and such built-in elements as the spiral staircase and the railing of the library and study above the living room. Despite the severity of the setting, the details all add up to an atmosphere of warmth and comfort. On the lower floor of the large main room (plate 234) two seating groups—a sunken one in front of the fireplace, another along the window—complement and at the same time contrast with each other, offering quite different settings for relaxed sociability at different times of day. Evenings, the fireplace (plate 235) offers coziness, and the built-in bookcases promote a mood of quiet withdrawal. By day the large window offers both light and a view. Since the shelves do not cover the lower part of the wall, there is a large recess at either side of the fireplace area which contains supplementary indirect lighting. The red picture is hung slightly off center, making a striking effect when seen from the door (plate 233). There is even a sight gag: the head of the large polar bear skin glares up at one out of the conversation pit.

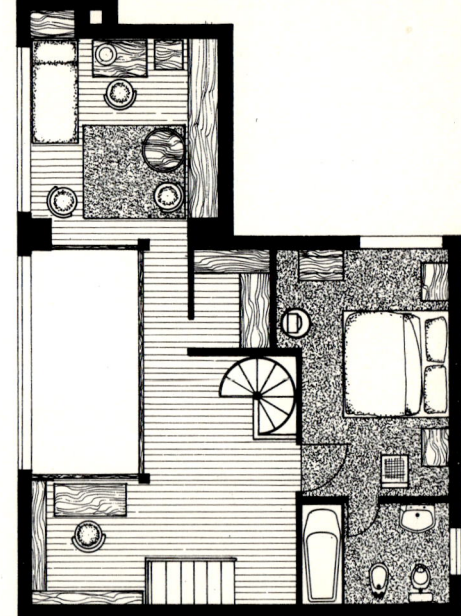

233a

233

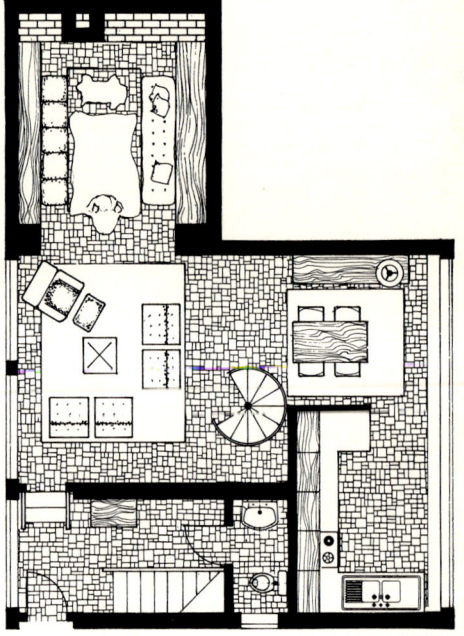

233b

234 ▶

156 The House as a Whole

235

236

The dining area lies off the living area and is separated from the kitchen only by a smoked-glass partition (plate 236). On the gallery (plate 237)—the railing is painted in a bold black-and-white design—there is a library with a desk and reading nook in front of the bookcase wall.

The bedroom is also kept in a quiet key and designed with great care (plate 238). Here the rustic character is toned down, though it is still present in the color scheme and in the pattern of the patchwork quilt, which complements that of the drop-leaf desk. The colors of this veneered antique desk, sliding door, and curtains are closely related and give a restful feeling to the small room.

239

240

239–43 White walls and ceilings, together with perfectly crafted built-in units, offer an ideal background for the fine furniture, art objects, and pictures in this apartment, which belongs to a New York designer. The core of the plan involves a combination of floor-to-ceiling closets and partitions, accessible from all sides, which also conceal structural piers. Throughout the apartment, large alcoves break up the wall surfaces and house either built-in wall closets, the white fronts of which keep them inconspicuous (plate 241), or bookcases (plate 242). Ledges in strategic positions hold sculptures, flowers, or pictures (plate 239). Set into the tops of some of the alcoves are broad translucent panels lit from above (plates 240, 241), and these provide such good illumination that only occasional ceiling spots and table lamps are needed. The living area (plates 239, 240) includes two conversation groups. Two easy chairs and a window seat comfortably fitted with a pad and pillows look out on Central Park; behind the grille concealing the radiator are the loud-

The House as a Whole

speakers of the stereo equipment. The conversation group in the alcove directly opposite the window was given an especially intimate character by building in a platform to serve as couch, extending the material of the floor covering over the platform and up the wall, and adding velvet cushions. The armchairs usually in front of the window can be moved when there are guests. On the other hand, the alcove is also a pleasant place for reading by oneself.

The two bedrooms are separated from the living area by doorless walls and built-in closets, without interfering with the overall flow of the space (plates 241, 243a); the guest room with its two beds can, however, be closed off by a folding door.

Apart from the living room and bedrooms, but linked with them by a long extension, are a large study and the kitchen. The study (plate 242) also serves as library and as an office in which to receive clients. Recesses with effectively placed works of art contrast with the bookshelves, some parts of which are also covered by pictures.

Its place preempted to make the study, the dining area was exiled to the kitchen (plate 243), which, small as it is, was ingeniously laid out to accommodate both functions with ease. All the indispensable utensils are stored in wall cabinets, and the working zone is kept in white to make it less conspicuous. The entire emphasis is on the dining area, which is agreeably furnished with pictures and with plants around the window.

241

242

243

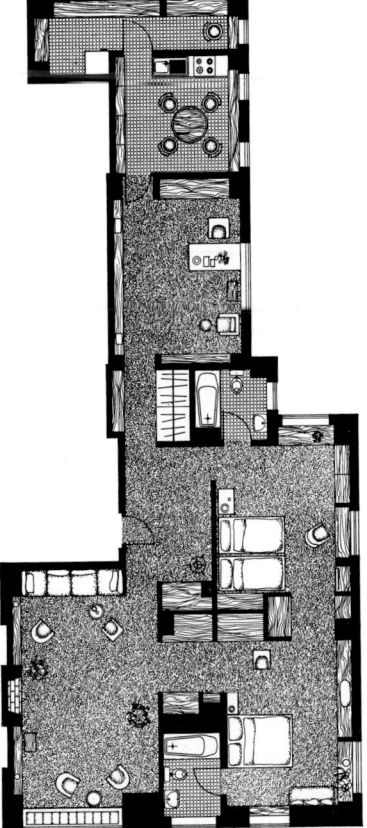
243a

160 The House as a Whole

244–47 In his own house, the Swedish architect Ralph Erskine combined traditional elements of the Swedish farmhouse with the uncompromising functionalism of contemporary architecture. Thus, for example, instead of lining up windows according to the usual symmetrical scheme, he introduced them only where needed. A vaulted ceiling spans the main room with impressive effect. A cube housing the kitchen is set into the main room like a house within a house (plates 244, 247). The overall plan involves four levels, further accentuated by built-in elements such as an open wardrobe alcove, a low partition at the work area, and a freestanding fireplace. On the lowest level there is an extensive living and dining area (plates 245, 246), and the fireplace in the center of the room shows how a good formal solution can be arrived at on a purely functional basis without the slightest decorative detail. Besides the large seating group adjacent to the fireplace, a second one was arranged directly in front of the window, together with built-in shelves for the radio, stereo, and books (plate 245). The dining area (plate 246) is conveniently close to the kitchen, and built into the wall between them are a serving hatch and shelves, accessible from both sides, and concealed by movable panels. The work area lies two steps higher, and from it stairs go up to the bedroom and other rooms. The main entrance opens onto a level area over the kitchen cube, from which the entire interior can be surveyed like a landscape (plates 244, 247).

244

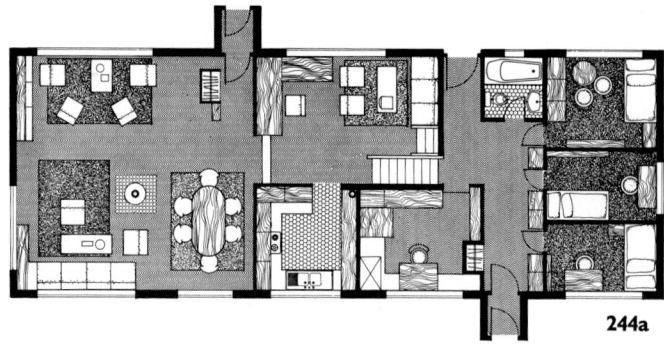
244a

247 ▶

245

246

The House as a Whole

162 The House as a Whole

248

249

250 ▶

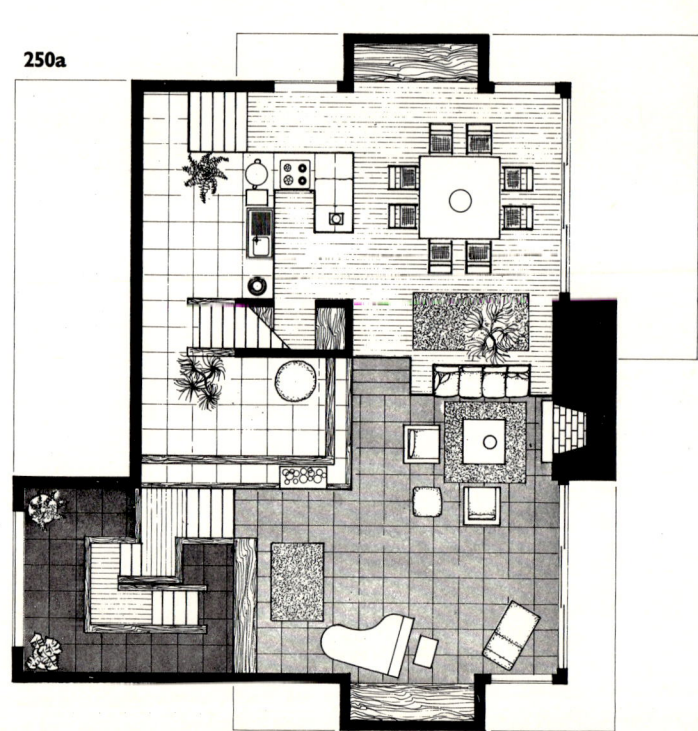

250a

248–50 This arrangement makes use of markedly different floor levels matched by different ceiling heights. In the living area (plate 250) the open timberwork gives the effect of a spacious hall, whereas the dining area and kitchen are of normal height (plate 250, background). By taking advantage of the differences in levels, a considerable amount of furnishings could be incorporated into the architecture itself. Another key factor in the overall effect is the warm-toned Douglas fir used for the walls, most of the floors, and the built-in furniture. The main room (plate 250) includes seating space, dining area, kitchen, and a gallery from which a staircase leads to the bedroom. The seating group is arranged around a fieldstone fireplace wall, and close by, in the base of the gallery, there is a bar with its own water supply to save steps back and forth to the kitchen. The dining area and the kitchen, adjacent to it, are intimately linked to the landscape by large window walls.

The kitchen is laid out in a U-shape and is defined only by the base of the gallery and two counters into which are built not only cabinets but also the stove, sink, and refrigerator, thus maintaining a close link to the dining and living zones. At the same time they remain inconspicuous, thanks to their perfect formal integration. The bedroom on the second floor (plate 248) and the children's room on the ground floor (plate 249) are also lined in spruce. A Navajo rug and a shag carpet give a touch of coziness to the large master bedroom, and a large outer deck and comfortable bucket chairs covered in bright red fabric make it more than just a place to sleep.

164 The House as a Whole

251–57 A unique collection of American postwar painting plus some fine pieces of furniture are the determining factors in the furnishing and arrangement of this New York apartment. As soon as we enter the reception area (plate 252), reached from a short entrance hall with a coat closet (plate 251), the large canvases of Arshile Gorky and Franz Kline command our attention. But though artworks play the dominant role, the apartment remains a home and not a museum, and furniture and artworks complement each other beautifully. With pictures of these dimensions, even museums have lighting problems; in a private dwelling such problems become even more difficult. Here, behind the molding of the dropped ceiling, there are concealed lights directed toward the individual paintings, and sunken spots in the living room ceiling. Understandably, the furniture had to be kept discreet in color and neutral in form. Consistent use was made of substitute pieces in dark wood and upholstery with quiet patterns; throughout the apartment these are matched by beige carpeting.

In the living room (plates 254, 255), which opens directly from the reception room (plate 253), the furniture is concentrated in the center in order to leave the walls free for paintings. Simple boxlike units surround the large couch on three sides and house part of the extensive reference library as well as the sound equipment. To avoid blocking the view of the pictures, all furniture and tables are kept low. The main focus of the room is the large canvas by Jackson Pollock, which almost covers the room divider set up between the living room and the dining area, with its equally fine paintings (plate 256). The collection also plays a role in the smaller bedroom (plate 257), where a long headboard behind the bed serves not only as night table and convenient shelf but also as a means of concealing a broad light source below the large painting by Bradley Walker Tomlin.

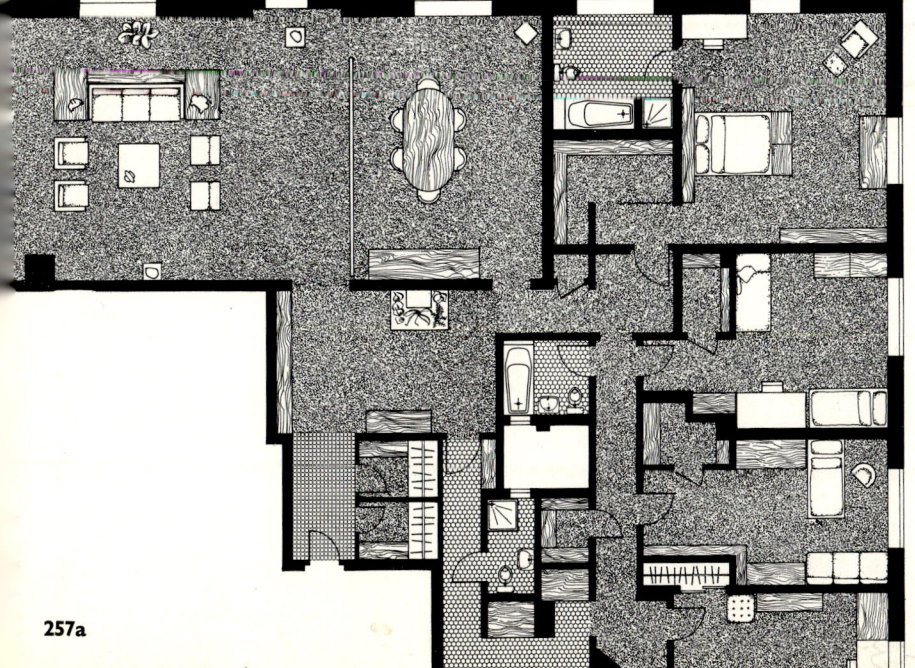

256

257a

257

INDEX OF ARCHITECTS AND DESIGNERS

All references are to plate numbers

Ammannati, Titina, and Vitelli, Gianpiero, Milan 154–56

Baldwin, Benjamin, New York 239–43
Bates, Harry, New York 31
Baughman, Milo, Provo, Utah 77
Beenhouwer, Owen, Lincoln, Mass. 141
Bloch, Mary, Humlebaek, Denmark 35
Boeri, Cini, Milan 64–67, 139, 182

Cagna, Oscar, and Lupi, Italo, Milan 211–14
Castellini, Piero, Milan 22, 68–69, 83, 115
Castiglioni, Achille, Milan 174
Catroux, François, Paris 34, 78
Cohen, Elaine Lustig, and Meier, Richard, New York 103
Colombo, Joe 73–74, 202–6
Conran, Terence, London 108
Copley, Nancy, Accord, N.Y. 144–45
Cromie, Victor, Cambridge, Mass. 120

Dini, Claudio, Milan 146
Dronneau, Jacques, Caudebec-lès-Elbeuf, France 134–35

Erskine, Ralph, Drottningholm, Sweden 244–47

FORMA, Paris 20, 87, 189–91
Fouquet, Patrick and Maïté, Bordeaux 136, 195–98
Frère, Jean-Pierre, Paris 51–53

Gautier-Delaye, Pierre, Paris 98
Genazzini, Giuseppe, Milan 5–6
Griffini, Ernesto, and Montagni, Dario, Milan 88
Guariche, Pierre, Paris 97

Hansen, Holger Tangaa, Lyngby, Denmark 179
Hardy, Hugh, New York 166–67
Hebey, Isabelle, Paris 180–81
Henriksen, Bard, Copenhagen 199–201

Jacobsen, Hugh N., Washington, D.C. 16, 46–47, 113, 131
Jaffe, Norman, New York 32, 248–50
Jones, Walk C., Memphis, Tennessee 133
Juvara, Romano, Milan 10

Kempen, Wim, Eindhoven, The Netherlands 75–76
Klinkenberg, Inge, and Maddalena De Padova, Milan 168–70
Kramer & Kramer, New York 251–57

Lagerfeld, Karl, Paris 7–8
Lago, Adalberto Dal, Milan 201–10
Lassen, Mogens, Klampenborg, Denmark 105–6
Lupi, Italo, and Cagna, Oscar, Milan 211–14

Magistretti, Vico, Milan 24, 36, 192–94
Mangiarotti, Angelo, Milan 147
Mazzuchelli, Tartaglino, Franco, Milan 41, 173
Meier, Richard, and Cohen, Elaine Lustig, New York 103
Montagni, Dario, and Griffini, Ernesto, Milan 88
Monzini, Rosanna, Milan 215–19

Moretti, Adriana and Gigi, Milan 176
Mortier, Michel, Paris 43, 99

Noyes, Elliot, New York 114, 123

Peduzzi Riva, Eleonora, Milan 61–63

Quintrand, Paul, Marseilles, France 93

Ravaioli, Carla, Milan 40
Ronchi, Milan 50, 70
Rossi, Fernando, Milan 11, 44, 45

Salier, Courtois, and Sadirac, Bordeaux, France 140, 230–32
Santi, Franca, Milan 192–94
Schöner, Wohnen, Hamburg, Germany 94, 109–10, 125, 138, 148, 153, 157–60, 177–78, 187–88, 220–23
Stephenson, Sam, Dublin 27
Stevan, Cesare, Milan 39
Studio A4, Milan 12, 23

Talion, Roger, Paris 96

Udstad, Sig, New York 79–82

Venosta, Carla, Milan 29
Vitali, Milan 164
Vitelli, Gianpiero, and Ammannati, Titina, Milan 154–56

Wilkes & Faulkner, Washington, D.C. 1
Wolff, Poppy, New York 2, 85–86

zuhause, Hamburg, Germany 15, 89, 100–101, 107, 124, 171, 183–86, 224–29

ACKNOWLEDGMENTS

The author's thanks are due the following institutions, architects, and photographers for permission to reproduce their work:

Benedetti, Carla de, Milan 5, 6, 10–12, 22–24, 35–36, 39–41, 44–45, 61–63, 68–69, 83, 88, 115, 139, 146–47, 154–56, 168–70, 173–74, 176, 192–94, 201, 207–14, 215–19, 230–32
Boys, Michael, London 108
Brecht-Einzig Ltd, London 244–47

Cardot, Véra, and Joly, Pierre, Bures-sur-Yvette, France 93

DLW, Bietigheim, Germany 3–4, 102, 150, 165
domus, Milan (Photo: Giorgio Casali, Milan) 202–6
Dressler, Fritz, Warmbronn, Germany 84, 90–91, 126–29, 162–63

Fioravanti, Alberto, Milan 30

Georges, Alexandre, Pomona, N.Y. 32, 79–82, 133
Guariche, Pierre, Paris 97

House & Garden, The Condé Nast Publications, Inc., New York: Bill Maris 116–17, 122 (all copyright © 1971 by Condé Nast Publications, Inc.), Massey 77 (copyright © 1969 by Condé Nast Publications, Inc.), Tom Yee 104 (copyright © 1969 by Condé Nast Publications, Inc.)

Interiors, Whitney Publications, Inc., New York (Photo: Robert Galbraith, Jamaica, N.Y.) 144–45 (both copyright © 1971 by Whitney Publications, Inc.)

Jaffe, Norman, New York 248–50
Joly, Pierre, and Cardot, Véra, Bures-sur-Yvette, France 93

Leloir, Jean-Pierre, Paris 43, 99, 134–35

Maison Française, Paris:
C.F.E. 98
Jean-Pierre Leloir 134–35
Michel Nahmias 105–6
Alberto Pinto 140
Foto Masera, Milan 50, 70, 164, 182
Maywald, W., Paris 9, 25, 38, 42, 51–53, 59–60, 71–72, 95
McGrath, Norman, New York 1, 16, 27, 46–47, 113, 120, 131, 141, 166–67

Namuth, Hans, New York 31, 114, 123
Nyqvist, Aulis, Helsinki 152

Palot, Georges, Paris 20–21, 34, 87, 96, 130, 137, 189–91
Photographis, J. E. de Trentinian, Paris 7–8, 17–18, 73–74, 180–81
Pinto, Alberto, Paris 13–14, 19, 26, 28–29, 33, 19, 54–58, 64–67, 78, 92, 118–19, 132, 136, 140, 195–98, 233–38

Reens, Louis, New York 2, 85–86, 103, 239–43, 251–57

Schöner, Wohnen, Hamburg, Germany 75–76, 94, 109–10, 125, 138, 148, 153, 157–60, 177–78, 187–88, 220–23
Shunk-Kender, New York 37, 161
Strüwing, Jørgen, Birkerød, Denmark 179, 199–201
Suomen Kuvapalvelu Oy, Helsinki, Finland:
Arto Hallakorpi 48, 111–12, 142–43, 149, 151
Mikko Julkunen 121
Jouko Levanto 172, 175

zuhause, Hamburg, Germany 15, 89, 100–101, 107, 124, 171, 183–86, 224–29

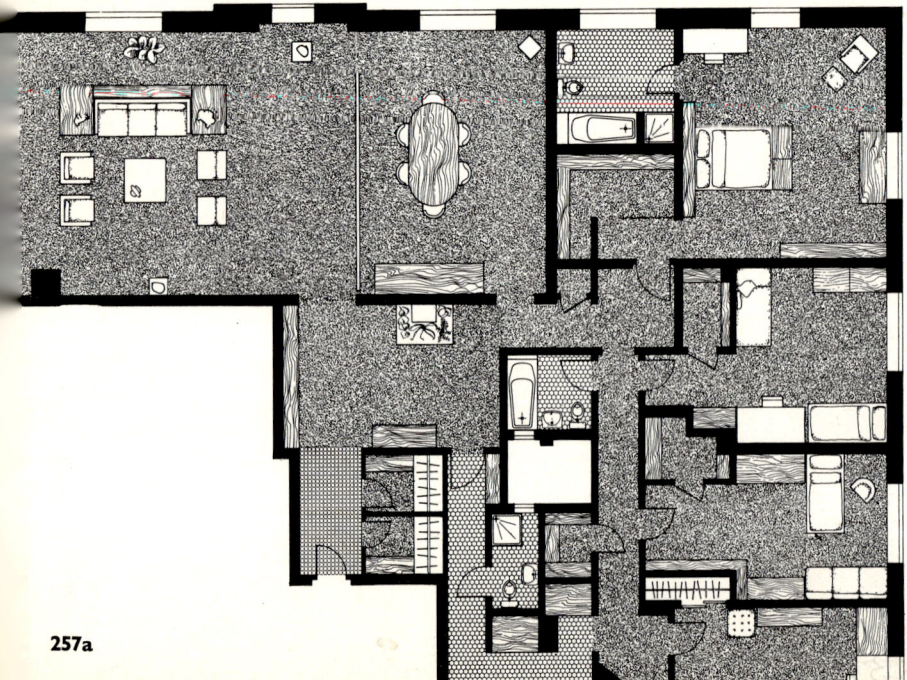

256

257a

257